VISION AND TACTICS

VISION AND TACTICS

Toward an Adult Church

GABRIEL MORAN, F.S.C.

HERDER AND HERDER

1968
HERDER AND HERDER NEW YORK
232 Madison Avenue, New York 10016

Nihil obstat: Brendan W. Lawlor, Censor Librorum
Imprimatur: ✠ Robert F. Joyce, Bishop of Burlington
February 13, 1968

Contents

A# 173

VISION AND TACTICS

Introduction

WE NEED in the church today a coalition of visionaries and tacticians. Taken separately, either one of these groups is dangerous; together they are an indomitable force for the good. I doubt that there are many people who are highly gifted in both ways. That is not so bad, however, since the improvement of religious education is a communal task. Each of us needs only to make a small contribution provided that we have the patience and the understanding to work with people on an entirely different wave length.

The sad thing is that we usually turn out to be neither theoretical nor practical. Our theories are not profound enough because we do not trust thinking and theorizing. But strangely enough, our practical advice is not practical either because we do not trust our experience. Instead of sticking with our strength we apologize for what we are or pretend to be what we are not. We make theoretical statements that are intended to sound practical or we give practical directions that are uselessly encumbered by watered down theory.

This book is mostly about vision, the kind of vision that contemporary theology can provide for religious education. There are also a few tactical moves suggested, particularly in the last two essays. Three reasons account for the imbalance in the treatment of the two concerns of the title. First, the catechetical movement has been deficient in having any theological vision to guide it. It is my thesis throughout these essays that the help of theology is what is most desperately lacking in religious education.

Second, my own competence is that of a theologian and this

9

is all that I can offer. It is constantly demanded of me that I explain how to teach religion to little children. My reply is that I do not know and I have never claimed that I did. This admitted limitation may invalidate everything that follows. I can only ask the reader to give a careful reading before making such a judgment.

Third, there is less space given to tactics because there is need for only a few of them. Having many tactics will not be especially helpful and may actually be confusing. The significance of tactics is that one does not talk about them, one does them to see what comes next. If the word "tactics" has a forceful, political, even military connotation, this is exactly what is intended.

Talking a great deal about the implementation of theories is seldom to the point. If real vision exists, it will almost always be correlated with a few tactical moves. This is the meaning of Kurt Lewin's well-known statement that "nothing is so practical as a good theory." It is why the visionaries and tacticians can meet; good theory and good practice do interrelate. The highly theoretical man and the very practical man tend to respect each other's work but not to imitate each other. If this does not always seem to hold true, I would suggest that a main criterion for judging a man's theoretical or practical capabilities is the respect he has for people doing the opposite kind of work from his.

One of those rare individuals who seem able to combine the visionary and the tactical is the architect Constantinos Doxiadis. Concerning the urgent task of city planning, he writes:

When building around the world, we are always confronted by those who want to think more, to express greater doubts, and think again; but these are not the philosophers, because if they were, they should have been guided on a path of action that was directed by careful thought. As things stand at present, humanity pays for this lack of conceptualization and action by seeing nature destroyed and

10

man left to suffer in an inhuman urban world. I can only represent myself in my capacity as a bricklayer—a mason and a builder. As such I can only conclude in my way that by avoiding action, we are drifting toward chaos! Let us act and build a human cosmos. We know enough to start; the remaining tasks we can learn only on the building site.[1]

In the field of religious education we need men on the building site carrying out carefully planned experiments. Without grass-roots operations nothing new and great will ever come to pass. But we also need careful planning at the highest and most general levels. This, too, is difficult work requiring intelligence, skill, effort and courage. Each of these two levels of acting is necessary for the existence and support of the other. The two of them are constantly moving toward each other but often it is gropingly through the dark.

Because neither of these two operations is self-sufficient, both of them are accused of being unrealistic. They are easy targets for people who pride themselves on their realism. What is the use of visionary planning when the hard practical realities remain unchanged? Conversely, what is the use of making one, good concrete change when the system is in need of overhaul and is liable at any moment to stifle initiative? Nearly everyone feels caught in a situation not of his choosing in which he is powerless not only to change the system but to find anyone who conceivably could. The inevitable tendency is to complain about the way things are but not to try for any great change. The result is a good bit of carping in the church that does not produce any positive suggestions. The critic need not come up with a solution but only with an element in an alternative way of acting.

Nearly all of the essays in this collection have been published before, though I have revised several of them. A reason for publishing them in book form is simply to have them in one place in one order rather than in the scattered places they

1. *The New World of Urban Man* (Philadelphia, 1965), p. 75.

originally appeared. But in addition, the subtitle of the book indicates that there is a unifying theme running throughout them. The vision and the tactics are designed to move the church toward an adult focus in religious education.

When I published my *Catechesis of Revelation* less than two years ago, I said in the introduction that it was a book mostly about children because that is the way things presently are in the church. I went on to say, however, that if one took seriously the theology presupposed in the book one might conclude that the whole focus of catechetics should be shifted from children to adults. In the last few years this has become more and more the dominant note of my own thinking. The same could also be said of many other people concerned with religious education in the country. As a matter of fact, "adult education" is one of the most frequently mentioned topics these days at catechetical meetings.

Although there is this increased talk about education for adults, yet it is very doubtful that the point has really been made. It is disconcerting to hear adult education listed as one of half a dozen projects that need attending after Catholic schools and CCD programs are taken care of. It is also not very helpful to talk as though fifty million adults are soon to be organized into little discussion groups and that these will work magic.

Most administrators who speak about adult education are thinking of taking the existing system and extending it beyond its present limits. I do not believe that we shall get very far until we begin thinking of this work as starting at the other end. The church's organized, educational resources ought to be at the service of the adult community. Whatever remains would be extended into the world of the child, but the child's main education would come via his parents. I am not naïvely unaware that this arrangement would require an institutional revolution almost beyond imagination. Nevertheless, we can begin to change the theological vision whatever be the institutional realities. As I have claimed above, if we had the vision we would find some concrete steps to initiate the change that might take a generation to accomplish.

My theological supposition is that Christianity is a religion for people attaining adulthood both in years and maturity. This is not to say that everyone else is excluded; we might all find ourselves outside. It is simply to say that Christianity is defined from its adult model and that Christianity of its nature demands that people grow up. In this way persons can better understand and more freely accept (or reject) Christianity. I am not positive that no other religion can be called an adult religion. However, extensive studies have shown that religions have usually functioned by appealing to the childish in man. Unfortunately, Christianity has often given the impression of doing the same thing. Its educational premise has been: Build up a wall while they are small and hope that they can hang on to their faith.

My claim on the basis of theology is that this is a completely false premise. Christianity is to free human intelligence for constant, never ending growth in belief. Thus, my advocacy of adult-centered catechesis is not a question of peripheral changes in organization, even less a matter of current fad. The adult focus refers to what I understand to be the essence of Christianity. Although many people say things that seem to be in agreement with this principle, things said in the next breath cast doubt on whether the principle has been grasped at all. Until there is much deeper theological insight among the decision makers, the needed reversal will never begin. In this introduction it is impossible to expound the theology of which I speak. However, there are well-established positions on the theology of faith and revelation, grace and salvation, church and authority, that are still not operative in this field. I am not only saying that these developments have not seeped down to the great numbers of Catholic laity; I am saying they have not seeped up to many of those in key positions who make policy decisions in religious education.

As to the tactical moves feasible at this time, there are but a few modest proposals in these pages. What is most needed at present, I believe, is some escape from the dilemma of Catholic school versus CCD. No one wishes to have this opposition but it is there nonetheless in the competition for talent, facilities, money and interest. In many places in the country there are heroic efforts being made in hopeless CCD programs. People bemoan the fact and talk about changing the situation but not much happens. The obvious reason for this is that the church has committed its educational resources elsewhere. Even when one does not intend it, serious talk about change in CCD inevitably sounds like an attack upon Catholic schools.

The hope that is currently on the horizon is the experimentation to create new approaches to religious education. Some of these experiments are taking place among a few families in a neighborhood, some are at the parochial level, a few are on a regional level. The underlying unity of these formal and informal ways to education is the proposal of an alternative to constructing more classrooms for children. There is no denial here of the value of Catholic schools or CCD and no call for their destruction; rather, it is a matter of concrete experimentation that will give positive help for an improvement of the total educational picture.

As part of this experimental movement I have urged that each heavily populated area have a center for religious education. This would not be a school building so much as a place where people could meet and where communication could occur. A place will not solve the educational problems but it would give a focus to efforts. It would give some sense of coordination to this work whereas at present one often feels frustrated by the fragmented and scattered use of resources. The investment of money and manpower would not have to be great in order to initiate such experiments.

I have said that one advantage of these experiments is that they can begin immediately without being proposed as a direct threat to either Catholic school or existing CCD. It must be admitted, however, that a meaningful experiment, almost by definition, will shake up and change the existing institutions. The firm decision to experiment in some serious way means that the institution has already changed fundamentally and can never be the same again. This holds true even if the particular experiment should later be judged a failure. If programs for the adults of an area were given strong support, they would eventually begin to reorientate the whole child-centered church. One should clearly recognize at the start, therefore, that a point of crisis will come sooner or later. But the problem in most places is getting a meaningful experiment going at all.

A further help in making progress would be to distinguish the various tasks which the church is engaged in relative to the educational field. "Catholic education" is a very ambiguous phrase. It can be and is used to refer to: (1) the Catholic church's involvement in education, (2) the education of people who are Catholics, (3) the education in what it means to be a Catholic. When these distinctions are not recognized it is assumed that, though Catholic education is wider than Catholic schools, a good Catholic school must obviously be a contribution to Catholic education.

I would claim that this is not necessarily true. The relationships among the three operations distinguished above are more complex than is usually thought. It may happen that the attempt to carry out one of these is the main obstacle to achieving another. For example, a school built in suburbia for the education of Catholic children may stand in the way of education in Catholic belief. If and when such a school exists, the feverish attempt to improve its religion teaching is utterly useless. It is the *existence* of the school, not the poor content of the curriculum, that needs changing. I am not saying that all of the church's schools or even all of her suburban schools are of this character. Schools must be examined one by one to see if they should continue to be, should close their doors, or should radically change into something else. This last possibility is

15

often overlooked in arguments over whether to keep the system open or to close it down. As part of the larger educational revolution, a school could, over a long period of time, change into the kind of center I referred to above. The immediate step in that direction may simply be finding ways to get parents more involved with the education of their children.

My remarks are by no means meant as a blanket attack upon the schools. I am merely asking school administrators to challenge their working premise, namely, that when schools are criticized the ready answer is that the schools can be improved. No one doubts that schools can be improved; the question is whether they should be. Where good public education is available, where the Catholic school is intentionally or unintentionally segregated in more ways than racially, and where other educational work is lagging for want of support, then the existence of the church-conducted school must be questioned. In this situation the question is not whether the church school can be maintained but whether out of service to the community and to the church it should not be closed. What must be asked is not whether the money is still available for maintaining schools but whether there are better alternative ways to expend resources.

This whole issue is sharpened by considering the church's mission to be among the poor of the earth and to serve their needs. The poor in our day and in our country are found mainly albeit not exclusively in the great urban centers. Any approach to social planning has to be done in a "metropolitan" context, that is, by considering the relationships of city to countryside, inner city to outer city. There is no hope for changing the decaying center of cities unless suburbia is also changing; policies that make the inner city what it is are dictated by people beyond the inner city.

This is an important consideration for the church's efforts in education. The issue is not really faced by the cry: Move the church downtown and leave the suburbanite to captivity

16

if not to the outer realms of hell. The church should indeed have much more of her resources at the service of the downtrodden and hopeless in the cities. The church should be there in dedication and strength far beyond the few heroic individuals who are now carrying the burden. While advocating this strategy, however, I would emphasize two points: (1) As many concerned Christians are present among the poor and downtrodden, other concerned Christians must be working to change the ethical-religious convictions of the affluent and socially comfortable. This is necessary both because suburbanites have souls and because this is the long-range way to change the conditions of the slums. (2) The church's function in the city today is not so much to conduct good Catholic schools as to conduct good schools. This means, in light of my threefold division above, that there may be a tremendous need in some cities for "Catholic education," that is, schools provided by the Catholic church to serve those in need. What the church is doing in this situation is fulfilling the mission she has had over the centuries, namely, to provide help when no one else is taking care of a social need. If the nature of these schools is not understood, the wrong kind of demand may be made upon them. The question will be raised: Why run a Catholic school which is not producing good, practicing Catholics? The answer is that even if not a word is spoken about the church and her belief, this church-conducted school might be making an extremely important contribution.

The two last points are intended to illuminate the fact that we continue to lump together under the term "Catholic school," institutions having quite different reasons for existence. Criticism cannot really be directed against Catholic schools because that *kind* of thing no longer exists. The changing social scene has left the church with something she did not fully intend: institutions that cannot turn out Catholic products but might by that very fact have a greater reason for existence. If the fact were openly admitted, then there might be less bewailing of the church's plight and more rejoicing that the church can now serve without vested interest. The church's mission in many urban settings may be to provide the stabilizing and integrative element of a school. There is evidence that many church-conducted schools are in fact making this important social contribution.

It is precisely to continue her educational service that the church needs a fundamentally new approach to the religious education of the educated, church-going, affluent part of society. Among these people there is certainly need for the church to educate, but a church-conducted school may be the last thing that is needed. If the church is going to serve the poor, then she cannot spend vast amounts of money on a school system for the non-poor. There has to be available for those who wish it a cheaper, more efficient way of *religious* education, that is, an education in what it means to be a Christian. The changes in society are going to be accomplished by intelligent, trained adults. The specialized, high-powered theological education needed here has to arise from the work of small groups of adults. A school probably will not help and may even hinder such work.

I am aware that the tactical changes must be spelled out in more explicit detail than I am able to do in these essays. Sociologists and economists must certainly be asked for their help. But scientists can only work with the tools and data and context provided for them. It is not up to them to say what the church is or what it should be about in the world today. Thus, I return to the need for a Christian vision. We have the people, the interest, the dedication, the institutions and the money. What we need is to trust in the vision that springs from the mind of Christ and then move to the building site to experiment.

1. The Future of Catechetics

IN PROPER medieval fashion the first question to be asked about the catechetics of the future is not what it will be but whether it will be. The answer to that question is: I do not know. It all depends upon your definition of the word "catechetics." Assuming the most commonly understood meaning of the word, I would say that the fundamental problem of catechetics is that it exists.

There are three themes that will intertwine in my presentation. Undoubtedly there is much else that could be said of the future in this area but I am quite certain that these themes will characterize the coming era. Moreover, the three of them form a single, definite pattern. In the working out of this pattern the catechetical will become so integrated into the church's life that one will be able to say either that catechetics has ceased to exist or that the whole church has become catechetical.

The three points I shall deal with are the following: First, a brief consideration of what I call a new era of sophisticated methodology. The treatment of this point must be brief because the thesis maintains that it can be worked out in detail only within the consideration of the other two themes. Second, after dipping back into some of my theological presuppositions, I will speak of the relation between secular and religious realities. This central point of contemporary theology has had almost no effect in either Protestant or Catholic education. Third, I shall speak about the adult-centered character of religious education. As this shift in orientation occurs, catechetics will tend to become identical with theological education. The work of religious education will no longer be thought of as a refuge for second-class thinkers. One will no longer hear theologians say: I do not know anything about catechetics; I am a theologian. What the man who says this really means is that the sight of forty little children in school desks scares the wits out of him. But any theologian worth anything knows a great deal about insight and communication, how a person comes to believe and how one develops the intelligibility of his faith. When theologians begin to realize that the educational task is primarily with people their own size, then they will not be frightened away from this crucially important work of theirs.

We are now entering a new era of methodological concern. This is in no sense a return to the questions raised in an earlier phase of catechetics; it is a pushing ahead to a synthesis never before possible. Writers in the catechetical field usually refer to the first third of this century as the period of *method.* The teaching of religion was improved by the adoption of some rather obvious principles of educational psychology. It is usually said that the past third of a century has been characterized by the improvement of the *content* of religion teaching. Few people would deny that what is found in the average religion textbook today is a decided improvement over the contents of these books a few decades ago. Nevertheless, it may have been premature to suppose that this improvement of the content is the essence of the problem.

I suggest that the last third of the century will be concentrated upon questions that are neither of content nor of method. There is no single word to describe what is at issue. I used above the phrase "sophisticated methodological questions." If the word "methodology" were used here, it would have to carry the sense of a style of thinking and a way of communicating. This is miles removed from the earlier kind of questions on method but even further removed from the insertion of a new content. Much of the discussion on method has been useless because the pre-conditions of a teaching situation were inadequate or non-existent. The teacher's question of how to get his material across to students is part of a much larger problem that must be tackled if teachers are to have a fighting chance. But concentration upon content is also an inadequate approach. It is based upon the misconception that there is a content to Christianity which is separable from a way of living and communicating with others.

The question for the future, therefore, cannot be method or content. The question is the inner relationship of these two, both in human life and in Christian faith. In the whole field of educational theory there will be more concern for how a person thinks than what is held before the mind. Does the thinking originate creatively and is it moving toward more fruitful insights? Education will be concerned with helping a person to think in a manner that will enable him to find his own answers at a later time. Schools cannot provide answers to questions yet to be asked. Schools could provide a way to approach questions that will set a person in the direction of truth.

This educational principle is certainly applicable to religious education. In fact, I would claim that it is especially important here. A religion that includes belief in creation and incarnation is concerned with how man thinks about this world and how he goes about living and communicating with others. Christian faith is not a certain content but they way a people look toward God. This is not to deny the value of doctrinal elaborations in Christianity. But the worst enemy of orthodoxy is the short-circuiting of the process that leads there. We need a life-long methodology for moving in the direction of orthodox formulations.

This new kind of methodology, therefore, involves the large-scale changing of institutional patterns. For this job we need men who know the techniques of social change and who can get a job done efficiently. The present catechetical arrangement often stifles the enthusiasm and kills the initiative of the best teachers. Although there are many teachers doing a mag-

21

nificent job, there is also a tragic waste of human energies and institutional resources. I have no detailed blueprint for the future but I hope that what follows points in a definite direction for catechetical organization. Theology cannot give us the answers here but it might give us the courage to use our heads to find better ways to do this work. We also need the courage to let some things die.

My second point refers to the effect on religious education of the so-called secularity theme in Christian theology. As background I wish to indicate the roots of this movement in biblical and theological developments. My summary must be brief but I hope that it will indicate the basis for this theme in theology and some of the consequences that ineluctably follow.

I said above that the problem is not content or method but their inner relationship. One might say that throughout theology the fundamental change that has occurred is the giving of primacy to relationship. To think in a relational way is not so easy as one might at first assume. It requires an altogether different style of thinking. One could put this in sharper contrast by saying that it is impossible to start thinking relationally. A person begins by living relationally and then he can gradually bring his sense-intellectual perception to bear upon this way of life. It is a process that moves from experience toward conceptualization, from description to definition, although the concepts and definitions never get a firm grip around the lived reality.

It is important to be aware of this presupposition when we speak of Christian revelation. We do not speak of two things which happen to be brought into a relationship. Rather, the things or persons are by being related; to be is to be in relation. By the word "revelation" I mean the particular personal relationship of knowing and loving. This is the deepest, most intimate kind of knowing that makes human life human. Revelation can never be deposited in a place; it is what happens

22

between people. Without people there is no revelation and, less obviously, without revelation there are no people.

In this relationship of revelation there is always a reciprocity of giving and receiving. No one can give unless someone receives; no one can receive unless there is a giver. Furthermore, to be receptive is the primary form of self-giving. The direct object of the verb "reveal" is always the pronoun "oneself." By a valid extension we speak of revealing something or some fact, but what is ultimately revealed is some person. There is no special thing needed for the revelation of a self. Every act, every word, every gift is to some extent revelatory of the partners in exchange.

There is only one God and from the beginning he was revealing himself to man through everything that occurred. One cannot think of revelation as two compartments of truths, one natural and one supernatural; the former accessible to all men, the latter open only to Christians. The classical distinction between the natural and supernatural retains some validity but only within the unity of the relation between the one God and the one human community. In every revelatory moment, one might be able to distinguish a natural and a supernatural dimension. But it is through the whole of creation that the one Father of creation speaks to all of us.

Every man, therefore, is exposed to the light of God's revelation. This was true from the beginning; it is more obviously so since the time of Christ. I cannot be sure of how well any other person is responding to God's invitation. I cannot even be judge of myself. I cannot approach the non-believer or the child with the assumption that he has not been touched by God's grace. I cannot assume that my task is to fill an empty vessel or that I possess something with which the vessel is to be filled. I can only approach the other with an attitude of invitation that we take up the quest together for the God already active in our lives.

If all creation speaks of God, then God is revealed in the "letting be of being," that is, in things simply being themselves. The more that things are true to themselves, the more truly they reflect the glory of God. God's revelation is not a religious veneer on things nor a religious message to be injected into people.

Christian theology contends that there is no religious realm of life, precisely because all of life can reveal God. This is not a reductionist movement attempting to make Christianity palatable to contemporary man. It is rather a challenging of man's whole secular life. The Lord of history is the one who can meet us in any moment of history. No place is God's place, because every place can be the place wherein God meets man. The affirmation of the secular in all its integrity is not only compatible with Christianity; it is what helps to specify Christianity as distinct from other religions.

One must admit that there are great dangers in this current of modern theology. There are many attacks upon the religious in the name of the secular that are naïve and uncritical. The letting be of the secular is not at all a simple matter. Whatever else it is, the modern world is not purely secular. It has its own ideologies and superstitions. It is not enough to get rid of religious idols while assuming that history will advance with the growth of human freedom. Man constructs false gods faster than they can be killed. The Christian claims that the only alternative to false gods is the true God, the one who judges all history.

There is really very little danger of God getting killed off. There is, however, a dangerous tendency to identify God with the ideal of human striving. He then can easily become an abstract principle of unification. I believe that this movement is inevitable unless we combine what I have said so far with some of the concrete imagery that is available to us in the biblical tradition. In describing a God who speaks everywhere to everyone I have approached the issue in an order that is

24

the reverse of the bible. The bible first leads us to a God who speaks to one person at one moment in one place. Without this other pole to our consideration we are liable to find ourselves with a vague and misty God who no longer confronts us in any distinct and demanding way.

The God of Judaism and Christianity, whatever else we may say of him, is not a vague, abstract or general kind of God. He is utterly concrete and particular, described by the biblical writers in terms almost embarrassingly concrete. With one man he walked in a garden, with another he wrestled on a hill top. To one man he said: "Take your shoes off"; of him another man said: "He is my Father." At first glance this striking particularity seems incompatible with a God of the universal creation. The paradox lies in the fact that not only do these two not exclude each other; they necessarily are joined together. A God beyond the manipulative controls and halting failures of man is a God who can offer his purifying love in the concrete moments of a man's life. A God who freely creates the universe is liable to be met in the most down-to-earth ways that man could hardly suspect or anticipate. Men can say various things of the God of Israel but never can they say that he is just what we should have expected him to be.

The coming of Christ was surely not the end of the unexpected, surprising and incomprehensible in God. The completion or fulfillment of revelation does not signify that we now have crystal-clear knowledge of God. Revelation does not imply that even on a human level. The knowing between persons always leads to deeper mysteries of unknowability. A man loved exists in the wonder of love, is sustained by the power of love without comprehending what the love is or how it is at all possible in his case.

The incomprehensibility of love is pre-eminently true in the case of God's revelation to man. It does not become all tidied up and conceptually clear. Its one clear effect is the shattering of all pre-packaged religious concepts. This in itself is no small

25

revelation. Much is thereby forever and always excluded, such as doing violence to the dignity of another human being. But what is to be positively done as alternative can only be discovered one step at a time. For this task of transforming history we have the example of Christ's life and teaching. We have received the freedom to create new possibilities and we are given the responsibility to trust in God and man. Since God's revelation comes to full expression in human life, it is henceforth life with all its ambiguities and lack of rationability that becomes the norm. Although we are to use our intelligence to its utmost capacity to discern God's will for us, we can never be certain that we are not ninety-nine per cent wrong.

I hope that it can be seen from all this that a strong emphasis upon the secular can and should be joined with a highly developed christology. Or, if we put that more precisely, the notion of secularity implies the Trinity: the creative Father, the incarnate Word, the transforming Spirit. This trinitarian God would not stand in contradiction to secular realities. A Christianity that has only a Jesus who is a very good man will become today just one form of secular humanism. But a Christianity that reaffirms its belief in a God-man died and risen is quite capable of taking into itself the best of contemporary humanism. At the same time it would protect humanism against its own destructive and demonic tendencies.

Revelation is what occurs in the flesh of each historical being. The light shines upon each man who comes into the world. Each man must find God in the world-line of his own history. God is still the God of Abraham, Isaac and Jacob, still the Father of our Lord Jesus Christ. He is still the God who has numbered the hairs of a man's head. The total, fleshly, social life of her people is what the church calls tradition and it is there that God's revelation is to be found. Far from denying the uniqueness of Christ, my assertion of God's continuing revelation in the church is an act of faith in the risen Lord as the norm of the whole of world history.

I have gone off on this theological excursion so that what follows will be understood to have a fairly solid foundation. What is soon to happen in religious education will not be an *ad hoc* adaptation to current fads; even less will it be a selling out of Christianity to secularist philosophy. There will instead be a realization of what is implied for education by a developed theology of the secular. We have seen that the letting be of being is not so easy as it may sound. On a personal level it means confirming people in their own best possibilities. We know all too well that each of us to varying degrees does not wish to become the person he is. We cling to something else. Something finite tends to become divinized; a social fiction is taken seriously; history gets turned into ideology. Christianity, for its part, is to be an idol smasher that keeps the future open to all the human possibilities; it is to punch holes in the games people play. Twentieth-century movements support the view that the secular world will not remain secular without belief in God. Not any old god will do. It must be the God of the present and the God of the future, the one who meets us in Jesus Christ.

If our belief were more solidly anchored in Jesus as first-born from the dead, we would have the courage to let go of many outdated forms we are now clinging to in religious education. We do not have to kill them, all we have to do is stand back and let them fall. There is still so much plastering on of unnecessary doctrinal language and artificial modes of prayer. Much of this we have not examined to the extent of asking whether it is alive or whether it is simply left over from another time and place. I am not proposing revolutionary discontinuity with the past. I am, on the contrary, asking for the kind of radical and critical examination that will preserve our deepest tradition. Whatever may have been true in the past, the preservation of dead forms of religious expression will in the future not only be useless to faith but will be an obstacle to it.

A world has emerged that is trying very hard to find its

sufficiency within itself. A religious educator in the midst of this struggle must be a man very much aware of ambivalence. He must see the real advantages and the great possibilities inherent in the secularizing process. Whereas many religious questions in the past teaching were simply distractions, the main issue of confrontation with God will emerge more clearly in the future. This is undoubtedly progress. On the other hand, the Christian teacher must be aware of the chronic sickness that affects this supposedly mature age. In the midst of sophistication there is a constant recurrence of superstition and a parasitical support from a Christianity supposedly rejected.

A Christian teacher of the future will use with great confidence all the best that is available in the art, literature and science of the day. He above all men should give these their full due. At the same time he will grasp them lightly so that they do not crumble in his hands. Every beautiful thing in God's creation could play a part in education to Christian life; but no one thing should swell up to become more than itself. The result of this kind of education is quite simply the recognition of creation as creation and the celebration that one is a creature of God.

This kind of program may sound like an education in bland generalities and abstract truths. Quite the contrary is being advocated here. The result indicated above can be achieved only by very specific and concrete experiences, the more deeply human the better. Every act of love, every appreciation of the gift of life, is a step toward the goal that Christianity points to. Can we not trust in the revelatory power of all good human experience? Can we not be patient with the verbal formulations that are specifically Christian? There is no touch of indifferentism here but instead a concern for the integrity of individual growth and the inviolability of personal freedom.

We see today that precisely because Christianity is concerned with the whole world and all peoples, then it is a religion which will probably be accepted by only a minority. Instead of spreading a thin Christianity over great masses of people, the work of Christian education is to give a real depth of understanding to those who freely accept Christianity. This is not a snobbish tendency. It is an attempt to work with those who are ready to give a witness to what Christianity is. Concerning the others who are not in this category, we make no judgments. We do believe that revelation is uniquely expressed in Jewish-Christian tradition. This does not imply, however, that Judaism and Christianity are the only ways nor even the most usual ways for man to go to God. The fact that the Christian no longer expects to convert the several billion non-Christians does not mean that he will be less concerned for them. On the contrary, the self-transcending message of his faith is that he must be concerned about the welfare of the whole world and that it is his enemies whom he must learn to love.

Catechetical work should therefore be able to proceed with calm patience and dedicated perseverance. Religious education ought to be free of a feverish concern for numbers and a desperate panic when our expected behavioral effects are not achieved. This is not to say that there should be no concern for quantity and results; but nothing is achieved without style and quality. In Gordon Allport's well-known study of the phenomenon of prejudice, he found that prejudice increases with a small increase in church going and religious education. With further religious involvement the prejudice will decrease. There could be varying interpretations of this fact but it at least shows the danger of a little, badly done education in Christian life. One could conceivably argue that unless catechizing is done thoroughly and well, it should not be done at all.

These considerations have already involved me in my third main point, namely, that Christianity is an adult religion. This follows from all that we have said about Christianity as a religion concerned with history, society, freedom and community. If this is the nature of Christianity, the teaching of it should be focused on the adult world. Furthermore, it is perhaps only a minority of adults who can profit from the formal course work. I said at the beginning of this paper that as education becomes adult centered, catechetical and theological education will tend toward identity. Religious education would then be directed to the groups of adults who are ready for highpowered theology.

My proposal here runs counter to a strong egalitarianism of today. There is a great demand for one clear and simple religious language that will speak to every single one of our contemporaries. I would maintain that this is not only an unrealizable ideal; it is not an ideal at all. Theology when highly developed can speak to only a few people and only in a somewhat technical language. There is a language of good popularization that speaks to a larger audience. But there are also vast crowds of people who cannot deal with language and ideas except in primitive ways. There is simply no way to reach such people with the formal learning of theology and catechetics. I think that we ought to stop trying. I am not disdainfully dismissing all the people who are unprepared for study. I am saying that we ought to play with them, pray with them, or do something about the conditions under which they are forced to live. But it is the destruction of theology and catechetics to expose the most profound notions of human existence in language that must compete with television commercials.

You may perhaps say that religious education is unavoidably in competition with television commercials and that we must learn to fight with the weapons of the competitor. I agree that there is a battle for people's attention and that we are probably not making the dent that we should be in modern means of communication. But I am certain that if we can only get across what we have to offer by trivializing and sensationalizing it, then the effort and achievement are in vain. The gospel does not fit congenially into the spirit of this or any other time. Our only hope is that people will recognize a different kind of need, a deeper form of desire, a different manner of questioning.

This is the inherent difficulty of Christianity and *a fortiori* of the teacher of Christian faith. He must be concerned with fidelity to a truth that is not at all obvious. As a result, he must risk giving the impression of creating something esoteric and removed from ordinary life. The vocation of the theologian is in this respect very similar to that of the artist. If the theologian is really speaking to the point and piercing through the trivia that inundate us, then he can be sure that he will not be heard by most people. For if his word can be immediately understood by everyone, it is probably not worth the saying.

We are rightly aware of a false elitism in which Christianity would retire into a gnostic ghetto. There is nonetheless a great necessity for small and elite groups. If members of such groups come to grips with Christianity they will not sit back congratulating each other for what they possess. They will be impelled by their study to be concerned with their neighbor. I admit to the continuing danger of such groups, but I maintain that this is no excuse for neglecting to form or encourage them. The ecumenical element that must from now on pervade all religious education provides good protection against the intellectual ghetto.

I realize that I have been speaking of religious education in a narrowly defined way. I know that there is a larger and less formal process that can go under the word "education." One could include in education not only the learning provided in schools but all the elements in a person's life that influence his psychological and intellectual growth. Jacques Barzun was referring to this larger process when he wrote: "Education is not merely schooling. It is a lifelong discipline of the individual by himself, encouraged by a reasonable opportunity to lead a

31

good life. Education here is synonymous with civilization. A civilized community is better than the jungle but civilization is a long slow process which cannot be 'given' in a short course."

In this over-all educative process the family has a central role. Likewise, in the total process of religious education, parents have not only a role but a primacy of position. I am always hesitant, however, to speak of parents as catechists or religion teachers. These words are likely to be understood according to the teacher-student model of the school. Parents educate not by being teachers but by being parents. The improvement of religious education is for this reason inseparable from the question of basic changes in ecclesial structure. All that is involved in that question cannot be dealt with here. But at the least it means an integration of the liturgy into the family setting in ways that go beyond what is being attempted now.

My reference to the family here is not a wistful and romantic plea to return to those good old days of the family (whenever they were). My remarks pertain to the future and I am quite realistic about the possibilities and limitations of family structure. I am fully aware that a nice, somewhat sheltered family atmosphere is not going to produce convinced Christian believers. The family is going to be less capable than ever of doing the whole job. But for that very reason the contribution it does make will grow more important. When much of society was modeled on family lines, there could more easily be substitution and overlapping of roles by civil and church agencies. In the future this will be less possible.

I am maintaining that in the future the family will have a more important contribution to make but at the same time will stand more in need of help from outside itself. This help will be primarily in the form of a continuing theological education for the parents. There is much to be done with children to introduce them to a Christian way of life, but there is very little that one can give them in a formal course of religion. We do not, therefore, begin by choosing between adults and children.

We begin by thinking of Christianity as a religion that can be truly understood and freely accepted only by the adult. After that, we teach adults as those who can grasp the Christian faith, and we teach children as those who are becoming adults. The most significant form of religious education for children will be, in Rabbi Heschel's phrase, the "cultivation of total sensitivity and man's capacity for radical amazement."

The kind of attitude that is leading toward theological questions is one which must suffuse the whole church and its educational structure. It is not something to be taught in either Catholic school religion classes or CCD courses. To what extent any formal courses on religion should be taught to children is a matter that needs further investigation. I hope that this question will be asked in conjunction with a search for means to introduce into public education the study of our Jewish and Christian religious heritage. In trying to deal with that delicate political issue, Catholics might learn something that pertains to the teaching of religion within the Catholic school. I refer to the fact that wherever religion is taught it ought to be done by competent teachers in an intellectually honest way and it ought to respect the individual's freedom by refraining from a proselytizing attitude.

I think that at present the schools are caught in a dilemma regarding the teaching of religion. This applies to CCD operations as well as the Catholic schools but it is in the latter that the problem is more acutely pressing. There is, on the one hand, a demand for good teaching and excellent courses with academic respectability. On the other hand, there is also a demand for unstructured approaches which speak of whatever is relevant at the moment and which let the students have their say. If and when students are ready to study Christianity, these two demands are not wholly incompatible. With children, however, the real teaching and study of Christianity must necessarily be brief. The relevancy desire is then served by spending the rest of the time on doing things for which schools are not specially suited. This uneasy alliance of aims in the school produces something that is neither intellectually challenging nor strikingly relevant. A concerted drive for relevancy succeeds only in proving how irrelevant schools are except when they are doing the job for which schools are built. The schools are going to have to make a choice here very soon because the problem is reaching enormous proportions. Timid and halting changes are causing the system to burst at the seams.

I am presuming that whatever be anyone's opinions, plans or visions, Catholic schools are going to continue to exist for a long time. This multi-billion-dollar reality could provide the setting for interesting and valuable experimentation. I am suggesting that insofar as religion remains a part of the school system, this is an area where innovation can be and needs to be tried. Up until recently the catechetical changes have been largely a matter of publishers selling new textbooks. Taken in isolation, this is a hopeless endeavor. That would be bad enough. But worse still, the impression can be created for a while that the new books are to some extent successful. They accomplish this illusion by watering down the latest theology. However, theology is not meant for little children; and the net result is an increase of the problems on a higher level of education. Later teaching of theology is largely an extension of the bad theology or a corrective effort upon what should never have been done in the first place.

I am not placing the blame for our problems upon the publishers or writers. They have tried to improve their materials while working in response to what the schools demand. Even less am I condemning the attempts of individual teachers in the system. I am saying that when one is faced with teaching religion to children every day in the present set-up, he is in an untenable position. He can avoid the subject and do something else or he can end up teaching a diluted theology. He will do the latter because there is nothing else to teach and he will do it rather badly because theology is not a subject meant for little children.

The way out of this dilemma is in the recognition that a much bigger revolution is at issue than the changing of content in curriculums or textbooks. A radical reduction in the quantity of direct religious instruction is an obvious need; but this must be done in connection with other experiments. Reducing the amount of instruction could be retrogressive unless there are guarantees that quality of instruction will improve. Thus, we need in the area of religious instruction experiments in the use of team teaching, large and small student groupings, multiple media of communication. The school administrator who objects to such experimentation on the ground that experiments in religion teaching would disrupt the existing school structure is quite correct. I am proposing that religion could lead the way in the revolution that must come to the whole educational system particularly as it extends into the adult world. That we do not have the personnel trained for this kind of creative work in religious education is painfully obvious. This situation could be changed in a relatively short period of time. But if those who are in charge of dioceses, schools and religious orders do not start a massive program of freeing their people for this purpose and giving them adequate financial support, the needed changes will never occur. The intelligent and dedicated layman, on whom the burden of the future primarily rests, can still get practically no financial help at all in the expensive process of becoming competent in this field.

Concerning the ultimate future of the Catholic school system, it is not my place to speculate. As we move forward with the kind of changes I have spoken of, we may conclude that Catholic schools should be eliminated, or what is more likely that we should make some distinctions not currently made between a system and various kinds of schools in the system. Likewise, within existing schools we may find that it is helpful to give religious instruction at several key points, or we may find that we should present it in many ways at many levels.

The present situation of the CCD also offers fantastic possibilities for change. Many fine things are being done with young people and adults. I would not wish to make a sweeping negative judgment. Nor would I advocate closing operations where vital programs exist. But in places where the resources are scarce and the odds insurmountable, is it not time to call a halt? What is achieved by going on doggedly while sending good money after bad? It is pointless to talk about extending a worthwhile educational program to adults after we try to reach all the children. If we wait for that time we will never get to the future. A reassessment of aims and means is necessary to establish rational and realistic priorities. Educational administrators could be helped by contemporary theology to face this issue. If theologians can manage to posit salvation outside the church, they can certainly find it outside the Catholic school and CCD.

I said at the beginning of this essay that the future will bring such a change in catechetics that we may say either that the field will cease to be or that it will be alive in much richer ways. Those of us who consider ourselves to be part of the catechetical field must decide on which direction we intend to move. In the one direction the catechetical concern will broaden out into work on the total educational process. This ultimately means a concern for church structures and for public education as well as church schools. The church will continue to have an important role in education particularly in caring for those whom society is neglecting.

The complementary pole for the Christian educator will be a highly specialized work. This will involve providing a high-quality theological education for those adults who are ready for it. The number who have the capability and the time for persuing theology may constitute a small minority. I do not think that it will necessarily always be that way. Even if it should be, however, the teacher who is reaching a few key people in society is making a significant contribution. The malaise we feel at present stems from our dim awareness that we are not working in either of the two directions that I have described. We are not with those who need us if they are to get any human education. On the other hand, we are not giving a specialized religious teaching to those who are ready to work for their society. When we are working only with the great numbers of people in between these two groups we feel superfluous. What we are doing is often being done as well or better by other agencies in secular society.

Much of the church's structure and much of our educational system seem to be falling all about us these days. Anyone not a little frightened by the upheaval would have to be foolhardy. There is no cause, however, for discouragement. Since the church's message is dynamite, Rosemary Houghton has written, the organization will always be in a state of partial demolition. A time of disintegration is a dangerous one, to be sure, but great risk and great opportunity are often coordinated.

A trinitarian revelation in which Christ is the norm and the Spirit continues to work in creation can have no final answers. This fluidity applies to catechetical organization as well as to theology. The very ambiguity and uncertainty of where we are to move from here is the reason for our hope. For there is not one obscure way that is the divine way, prefabricated for us in the past. There are thousands of divine ways that can be affirmed by us if only our imaginations are wide enough and our hearts are light enough. "For the last of all the mercies of God is that God is lighter than man" (Capon).

2. The Time for a Theology

ACROSS the country these days one finds among teachers of religion an amazing divergency of attitudes relative to the catechetical movement in the United States. These differences in attitude cut across the divisions of Catholic school and CCD, grade school and high school, young teachers and old teachers.

There is in the first place a large group of teachers (though the number is perhaps diminishing) who believe that nothing has really happened. These teachers feel that despite the flurry of new words and glossier textbooks the important thing is to stick to the solid, traditional doctrines they have always taught. There is a second group, also large in number, who have just caught the message. They now see the whole picture in one great sweeping vision. Their only question at catechetical meetings is how does one convince the old teachers that what they are doing is wrong and that they should adopt the "new approach."

There is also a third group of teachers which is small in number but growing rapidly. These are the teachers who have been through the "new approach" and who have become somewhat skeptical about it. They took to it with enthusiasm and skill; they found the students eager and waiting for this interesting new material. But they have been with it for a few years now and the students have been with it too. And the teachers have begun to suspect that all this new material is not connecting with the students' real lives. They have also begun to notice the pained expression on students' faces when someone starts "recounting the events of salvation history." This group of teachers is in the process of moving away from the "new approach" but they are not sure of what to use in its place. I have heard more than a few of these teachers in the past year describe their religion class in terms such as these: "I let the students say anything they want. We discuss their problems; we talk about movies and newspaper stories. We do anything that is meaningful and relevant." There is, finally, a fourth group of teachers probably few in number though they show up well at catechetical meetings. These are the teachers who are on the second wave. They have passed through the first enthusiasm for the "new approach and have met with some disappointment. They recognize very clearly that there is need for more subtlety and depth. They feel that they are now coming to grips with the hard facts of the matter. One hears them say at catechetical meetings: "Eichstätt spoke only of kerygma and catechesis but Bangkok pointed to the real need, namely, pre-evangelization"—a statement unintelligible to all but the initiates.

My intention is not to caricature these points of view nor to take up the defense of any one of them. I am trying simply to describe the situation that exists and to ask what all this means. I am not without some sympathy for each of the four attitudes described above. I think that it is very likely that each group perceives something of the true state of affairs in religious education today and something of what is needed. Perhaps these are four stages of development and the only thing we can do is wait until everyone catches up with the leaders, that is, with those in the fourth category who have the newest new approach to teaching religion. This could be so, but one must be suspicious. I have the uneasy feeling that there is too much grasping for immediate solutions. No matter what comes upon the scene it seems exposed to being trivialized into gimmicks. The tendency to trivialization, jargon and repeated frustration is, I maintain, no accidental occurrence. There cannot be solid and permanent advances in the teaching of religion without a thorough theological understanding of what catechetics is about.

It is my contention that the catechetical movement stands in desperate need of theological principles of self-criticism.

The thesis I have just proposed may sound old-fashioned or reactionary to some people. It is generally assumed that catechetics began to make progress when it separated itself from an encrusted theological system and began to speak in simple terms of God's plan of salvation presented in scripture and liturgy. The fact is correct enough but one must be careful about the conclusions that are drawn from this fact. It is true that catechetics needs to be historical and Christ-centered, scriptural and liturgical, social and pastoral; but so does Catholic theology. What many people writing in catechetics do not seem to grasp is that theology has been in a process of renewal similar to catechetics—only more so. Given the way things were, it was probably inevitable that the catechetical movement should have gone through an anti-theological phase in which it tried to solve its problems with scripture and liturgy. That day is now passed. It is theology which will make or break any catechetical movement.

My proposal obviously is not to set aside the great gains that have come from scriptural and liturgical developments. It is rather to integrate this material into a theological understanding of Christian revelation. Catechists do not have to start doing the work; it has already been done or is being done by leading theologians. What the catechetical movement must do is simply put aside the anti-theological bias which still pervades much writing on religion teaching. It is time for catechetics to recognize that theology is its chief ally and not an enemy or an estranged relative. It is time to put to definitive rest the implication that theological reflection is at best irrelevant and perhaps a bit dangerous to the Christian life. This, I would claim, is the real crisis of catechetics today: not the catechism and the theology manual which are dying, but the rising hope that the religious education of hundreds of millions of people in an incredibly complex world can be carried out with a dash of scripture and liturgy accompanied by much sincerity and good will. This simply is not enough. There is need for patient inquiry, deep understanding, and detailed knowledge. I point very briefly in this essay to two notions central to both theology and catechetics today. I suggest that the catechetical implications of these two could be more fruitfully realized if catechists would give more consideration to the theological analysis of them.

HISTORY

In contemporary catechetical writing there is great emphasis upon the historical character of Christian revelation. Teachers are constantly told that the only way to convey a true understanding of revelation is by presenting it as a "salvation history." When this is said, however, there is seldom advertence to the fact that the word "history" is so little understood that this statement may confuse the issue rather than clarify it. Despite all that has been written about history in the past century, most of us continue to work with a naïve concept of history. When we are asked to take that concept of history and modify it according to the peculiar demands of scriptural exegetes, it may be a strange concoction that comes out as "salvation history." When this elaborately conceived history is transferred to the students, it could easily happen that their conception of revelation will be more artificial, contrived, abstract, and irrelevant than their non-historical notion ever was.

If one asks why we should teach our Christian faith as a history, the obvious and immediate reply one receives is that this was God's method of teaching and that we should imitate him. It seems to be assumed that God was a rather effective teacher who chose to use good audio-visual aids and so conveyed his revelation through historical events. It thus becomes important for the religion teacher to line up the material

41

according to an historical sequence, to point out the great events of the plan, and to show how we received the revealed truths through the interpretation of the historical events. By presenting revelation as a story of events about God entering history we are supposedly making religion relevant to modern man because modern man is supposedly interested in history.

I certainly do not intend to deny that we should meditate upon God's method of teaching in order better to understand our own. Nevertheless, we must not confuse a starting point with a conclusion. Catechetical theory and methodology are not established simply by saying that God used history to teach and therefore we are to do the same. What is needed in catechetical writing is some realization of the complexity of the notion of history and the paradoxes inherent in a Christian understanding of history. This I fail to see in catechetical writing. I suspect that the meaning of history has hardly been touched here and that we are stirring up interest in historical presentation only to prepare for a bigger let-down. It is casually said in catechetical writing that God could have used many other ways to teach revelation but that he chose history as a good pedagogical tool. Such a statement, if not false, is theologically vapid and betrays the superficiality of our understanding of what is involved in an historical revelation.

What is of great concern to me is that theorizers on catechetics are showing even more of a preference for the past over the present than used to be true. No one who proposes to speak of Christianity can neglect considering the past, but the past ought to be taken up into the community of the present. The contemporary world does show some liking for history, but what contemporary men are especially interested in is the present historical evolution in which there emerges genuine novelty. To these men, a series of events in the past that delivered a set of revealed truths not only does not restore value to history but seems to be a direct denial of it. Ironically, therefore, the more that advocates of teaching religion as history talk, the more they convince many of their contemporaries that they are opposed to history. They are charged with not taking seriously man's present history.

It can hardly be denied that whatever religion textbooks may now and then say about the present, their point of concentration is clearly in the past. When it is a question of the present world, the task proposed to the student is the application of answers handed down from the past rather than the discovery of anything new in the present. Of course, it is repeatedly said that salvation history is still going on and the student is to participate in God's continuing plan of salvation. If one should challenge the meaning of this statement, the author would be quick to assert his orthodox belief that the divine, public revelation ended when St. John put down his pen. We are assured, however, that much else in God's plan continues to happen and that the student is to live now, to worship now, to love now, to be sanctified now. He is also allowed to develop more explicitly the closed revelation. The Christian student is thus encouraged to live in the present except that his mind must be pointed backward to where all the revealed truths are. This is an unhappy situation for the Christian, but it is hardest of all upon schools and religion classes whose function, one would suppose, is to raise the level of understanding in order to set men free. Schools cannot exercise their function unless they are allowed to focus on the real world of men and events and thus discover the truth in the world through the application of human intelligence. Unfortunately, the conception of revelation which is presupposed throughout catechetics prevents just such an openness to the present event. No one is more aware of this than the students. They know that whatever questioning and open discussion may be allowed in class the answers have already been given. By the end of class the cards must be laid upon the table.

Experienced teachers who are striving to make Christianity meaningful to students sense that there is something more to be said here but they are not sure of how to get beyond their difficulty. Those who have been writing in recent years in catechetics sense too that the "revealed truths" inserted into the students do not produce the desired results. Their solution has been to play down the role of knowledge and understanding even while insisting that knowledge has its place. Religion teaching, it is said, does not deal with mere knowledge and intellectual truth; there must be other things more vital added to the knowledge. The teachers are told that their task is not to instruct but to form their students. The "revealed truths" are hurried over as an awkward preamble to the real business of making one's students committed to Christ and fully formed persons.

The program is impressive and the end is desirable, but the means are destructive of the possibility of success. What is needed is not less emphasis upon revelation and intellectual understanding in favor of more practical tools, but rather more examination of the character of Christian revelation. The failure to wrestle theologically with this issue must inevitably result today in violence to personal freedom and in the self-destruction of the school's function. I am completely in favor of total Christian formation and commitment to Jesus, but I doubt that schools can do these things. What I would like to see is the schools and the catechists making a small but valuable contribution to the total Christian endeavor. What I particularly object to is that catechetics is neglecting the very thing it is capable of contributing, under the pretext that it has always accomplished that thing very well. It is practically a truism in catechetical writing that what was wrong with religion teaching in the past was that it was too intellectual and too much concerned with knowledge and understanding. I consider the statement an absurdity. The one way in which religion has almost never been taught has been by appealing to children's intelligences.

I claim that beneath these catechetical difficulties lurks the deeper issue of the relation between revelation and history. What is specific to Judaic-Christian revelation is its historical character; this means something more than its being written down in history books and put into charts in salvation history textbooks. An historical revelation means, first of all, that God enters into the real life of men, their bodily, spatio-temporal, social situations. Other religions tend to conceive of revelation as a collection of secret truths handed down by the gods and untouched by the temporal flow of existence. These are the dogmas and precepts to which men are to conform their lives so as to imitate the gods and find salvation by escaping from time. The real, changing, bodily life of men makes little difference; it is the unchanging, eternal reality which conforms to the revealed truths.

In an historical revelation God reveals not secrets about himself but himself. God reveals God not in the instant of some dim past but in the continuing human experience of the present. God takes to himself in revelatory relationship, not an inner spark of the eternal, but man—the temporal, bodily, social being. There is history to Christian revelation and there must always be history in religion teaching, not because God chose a good gimmick but because God chose man. He still chooses man so that the real history of today is the locus of the continuing revelation. Revelation never becomes a system of truths to confine man's life; it is the ever present invitation to man to open his life beyond himself and discover the perfection of freedom in relation to the one who is revealed. Revelation does take place in historical events, that is, in the concrete, personally experienced events of man's life; but such events are the present events of the person in community. God reveals and man believes; revelation can exist and continue to exist only in the present, personal interrelationship of God and mankind.

There is no way that one could put revelation into a book or an institution, though this is not to deny that writings and institutions might have an important role in the revelational

45

process. What has happened in the past in the interrelation of God and man has an indispensable role to play in understanding the present, but it is the present pointing to the future that is the focus of reflection for a prophet or for a religion teacher. God takes hold of each man with fundamental newness and it is in his own personally experienced history that each man must find God if he is ever to find God. The teaching of religion begins, therefore, with the student's own history within his own community. The student will not adequately understand that history until he sees it as part of God's cosmic dealing with the people of Israel, the humanity of Jesus Christ, the Christian community, and all mankind. Nevertheless, he cannot be attentive to the history of the world without first discovering the people and events of his own history. It is here that God is dimly but truly confronting him, holding out the communion of knowledge that we call revelation. An historical revelation, therefore, means that God is someone real who penetrates the real life of man, that man in his bodily-social existence is the one called; that a present personal interrelation exists between God and man. The meaning of this process is brought to light by understanding it with the help of all that the past tradition and the present community provide.

Much of the above has been said many times before in catechetical writing. The trouble is that catechetical writers are afraid to take seriously their own statements. They would like to mean it when they say that God is now speaking to the student. They would like to believe that the historical events of our experience are an opening to the understanding of God's revelation. Good teachers sense that the only way Christian faith can be personal and communal, the only way it can be the perfection of freedom rather than a restriction of life, is if it is a present happening which men discover in their lives through dialogue with others.

A revelation that really happens in the personal and free experience of men is precisely what Catholic teaching seems to deny. It seems to maintain that revelation was finished when Christ delivered the completed revelation to the apostles. Since the time of the apostles it would seem that revelation can come to men only in the form of truths announced to men from the outside. Despite the new vocabulary, the underlying conception of revelation is still one of *things* passed down from one generation to another and dutifully inserted into people by preachers and teachers. Whatever coverings and additions are made to the old concepts, there remains underneath a non-historical, non-social, impersonal understanding of revelation, inhibitive of growth and freedom, concerned not with a living God and living men but with a God who retired from the world leaving his truths behind him. The claim of catechists to be dealing with a present, personal, relevant Christianity does not stand up well because there is little theology provided to back up the words. If we are going to keep talking about encounter and commitment, either we ought to admit that we are just using pious phrases or else we ought to give the words some theological meaning and depth. The theological question is whether in fact Christian revelation can be a present, personal, social reality, and if so, how.

CHRIST

The key issue here as elsewhere in Catholic theology is the role of Jesus Christ. Only with an adequate Christology can there be provided a firm theological foundation for the teaching of Christian faith. It is repeatedly said these days in catechetical writing that Christ is the revelation of God, that in him revelation reaches its fullness and perfection. One might question, however, how well this statement is understood. I suspect that it is generally taken to be a beautiful metaphor indicating that through Christ's words and actions there was transmitted the full collection of revealed truths. Revelation

47

would still be understood to be *something* given to man, if not handed down from the heavens then delivered by a divine messenger. It would be thought that just as God acted in the events of the Old Testament to communicate truths, so he acted in a definitive way in Christ to teach us about himself. In this perspective the apostles would have the function of copying down the truths (with only a small degree of corruption) and storing them for use in the post-apostolic church.

The reduction of Christianity to one of many religions in which the revealed truths are handed down at the beginning inevitably happens if we do not sufficiently appreciate Christ's life, death, and resurrection. What distinguishes Christianity is not the belief that a divine being appeared on earth to pronounce the final revealed truths. What Christianity claims is that the Word has become flesh and that man is no longer alone before God. There is no salvation in clinging to secret truths but only in flesh being taken up into the freedom of a son. "It is in the flesh that salvation hinges" (Tertullian).

I have said that revelation is a personal communion in which man as the recipient stands within and not outside the process. God gives himself to man and man accepts this personal gift as the final boundless opening of his freedom. God gives himself in a special way to the people of Israel in their communal history. This history culminates in God's personal gift of self to the one who emerges from that history and the one in whom the history of Israel and of all men is recapitulated.

Jesus Christ is the revelation of God not solely because God acts in him but because he is the communion of God and man. Without the human recipient there is no revelation and it is precisely in the human understanding of Jesus that revelation was perfectly received. In his understanding there was gradually attained a never-to-be-surpassed revelation of the Father and his will for mankind. There is a sense in which all was given to Christ from the start; he did not become divine nor did he wake up one day to discover he was God. Catholic faith maintains that Jesus was never entirely lacking in the knowledge of who he was and what his mission was. There is a difference, however, between a global awareness of self and a detailed, reflexive, communicable knowledge. It was in his own human history that Jesus grew into the fully personal knowledge that constitutes the perfected revelation. Contrary to what is usually assumed, the revelation of God in its completeness is given not to the apostles but to Jesus Christ. He is the perfect union of God and man, the one in whom the loving Word from the Father meets the complete receptivity of human understanding and freedom.

The development of Christ's knowledge was a lifelong process. Advancing in wisdom and favor, he learned obedience by the things he suffered and sealed his life with the acceptance of death. Opening himself to the total transformation of the spirit he became the perfect recipient of God's revealing and redeeming love. At the resurrection the revelational process reached a high point never to be surpassed; but this was not the end of revelation, it was its beginning in fullness. What distinguishes the process now is that Christ has taken up a definitive relation to all men. All of human life can henceforth be revelational of God. The Spirit has become the law and norm of Christian life, not in doing away with all external structure but in giving an understanding of Christ's words and their embodiment in mankind. Revelation is not a patchwork of external objects and inner lights but a personal communion in Christ with all who are united to Christ.

The revelation in Christianity comes to its end in Christ but Christ does not end. He continues to receive from the Father and to share his knowledge with his Church. The main reason why Catholic theology has hesitated to speak of a present happening of revelation has been because revelation was not related to the risen Christ. There is no question here of going beyond Christ or adding "revealed truths" to the deposit of faith. What is necessary is that the Church live in history sharing in the history of Christ's revelation from the Father. It is, therefore, in the events of the Church's life (with the liturgy as the epitome of her other activities) and in all the events of world history that the Church now learns what God is now asking of her. There is a genuine search after the truth wherever it is to be found, without *a priori* limits but aided by all that human reason and Christian tradition can supply. The Church is not called to work in a boxed-in area of logic applied to scripture. Instead, the Church's mission includes reflection upon all that is human to understand how the human is to go beyond itself.

The scriptural testimony to the one who received the fullness of revelation has an indispensable and indefectible role to play in the reflection upon humanity, its capabilities, and its end. The early Church determined and fixed unchangeable these testimonies, not to end revelation but to make its safe continuance possible. The "closing of the deposit" guarantees the objective element in the past precisely so that the Church can live in the present and concentrate on the future. While it is legitimate to refer to scripture as the expression of God's revelation, the full meaning of revelation must be grasped by beginning with the intercommunion of God and man. Strictly speaking, therefore, revelation is found in completeness in neither scripture nor tradition but in the human consciousness of the risen Lord.

The Christian paradox of the once-for-all accomplishment in the past and the continuing working out of the process in the present applies throughout Catholic theology. It is particularly important in this question of revelation. There is obviously a sense in which God speaks a definitive or final word in the life and death of his Son. It should be just as obvious, however, that God is still speaking in this world through his Son, for until the community is formed his body is not yet complete. Revelation continues to happen not primarily because a "Christ event" can transcend time, nor because the Word is preached nor because the Church teaches apostolic truths. All these have their place but what is first is the continuing communion of the Father's Word with the glorified Lord who heads humanity.

CATECHETICAL CONCLUSIONS

The main issue that arises in the minds of students today when one tries to teach them religion is the question of freedom. Catechetical theorists may not like the fact, but it is the fact from which they must start. This issue of freedom does not suddenly develop at the point at which the student can articulate his desire of and his demand for freedom. The sense of personal autonomy and human development is an all-pervasive force spreading throughout the world among all people and age groups. A reflexive awareness of the necessity of personal freedom has not yet reached every part of the world, but certainly anyone exposed to education in contemporary American society can hardly remain untouched by this development.

It is a source of amazement to me how blithely unaware of this fact much catechetical writing seems to be. The de-emphasis of intellectual understanding in favor of other techniques of formation does violence to the personal freedom of students and leads catechetics to neglect the very thing which schools are capable of contributing to the growth of freedom. The way in which the teacher respects the person of another is to seek for a communion of understanding with the other that will provide the possibility of his taking up his own freedom. There is no direct way to form another human being's freedom; all that one can do is provide the context and the love and the light of understanding. Much of the newest catechetical writing, instead of presenting the broad human context from which a Christian understanding could slowly emerge, is ridiculously direct in its attempt to mold people. There inevitably appears in this a thinly disguised salesmanship which seldom fools any of the students.

51

This theme of freedom is involved in all the catechetical questions today. For example, in questions of curriculum construction it is usually assumed that there are students on one side and there is a body of revelation on the other side. The problem becomes how to match the one with the other so as to get this body of material inserted into the people. It is thought that either one can attend primarily to the development of the student and thus structure the teaching psychologically or else one can follow the order of revelation and arrange the course material theologically. This conception of things is not quite accurate, and to the extent to which it is faulty it will lead to the opposing of human freedom rather than its genuine development.

It is true that there is a distinction between the people who are the Church and the objective elements that are inherent to the notion of a Church. But this distinction is one between poles in a single revelatory process and not between people and revelation. There is no revelation except in God revealing himself in personal experience. In deciding on the basis of a religion curriculum it simply is not true that one should choose (or could choose) either the child or the revelation. One must structure the teaching according to the people precisely because that is where revelation is. Why do not catechetical writers take seriously their own profession that God's revelation is found in Jesus Christ and his brethren instead of immediately reverting to the identification of revelation with doctrines? In the teaching of religion one must begin with the students, not because this is easier psychologically but because this is better theologically. This principle does not mean that the objective elements of Christian revelation are to be disregarded. They are to function in teaching as they function in the revelational process, that is, they are the means to express and to understand God's revelation of himself in human life. But it is life and revelation that are to be understood.

The focus of religion teaching, therefore, is the community

of students and teacher as open to the wider community of man before God. The means for teaching the Christian religion is anything that is human, anything that can contribute to the true perfection of freedom. This proposal has nothing to do with a closed-in secular humanism; it is, on the contrary, based on the assumption that the human has been taken into a new relationship in Christ and that the whole world is to be his body.

Recent catechetical writing has been taking it as axiomatic that there are four ways or four signs for teaching religion: scripture, liturgy, doctrine, witness. Though these are obviously sources and means for the catechist's work, the attempt to structure all religion teaching according to these categories is unfortunate. There is an inevitable tendency to trivialize these great realities and there is also rapidly growing up a new rigidity and narrowness. There are not four ways, there are innumerable ways to teach Christianity, all of them finally converging in the single access to the Father through the Son. As the theological preparation of teachers improves, the ways of teaching religion will multiply. If such preparation of teachers cannot be immediately provided there is still no point in narrowing their minds into four pre-set categories. A teacher might find that a novel, a movie or a cartoon strip is effective in throwing some light upon the Christian meaning of life. He ought to be allowed and encouraged to use such material, not as a psychological prop for inserting "revealed truths," but as a theological aid to help men to understand what it means to be truly free. The question for teachers is whether they really believe that every step toward truth and freedom is a step toward community in Christ. And it is one thing to say nice phrases like this; it is another to grasp with some depth of understanding what the whole issue is and what the possibilities, limitations and dangers are.

This advocacy of a reflection upon the present, personal history of the student is not to be understood as a superficial "problem centered" teaching of religion. In this latter case, the supposed problems of the students are discussed and answered with solutions taken from the bible or the Church's teaching. This way of catechizing shows a lack of respect both for the Church's teaching and the person of the student. The center of concern ought not to be the isolated individual and what he thinks are his big problems. Christ did not come around distributing solutions to problems, least of all the problems of adolescents. Christ came and lived human life to the end, and he invited men to grow up in him. It is in the real world of men and events confronting the student that God is revealing today. Consideration ought to be directed, not to the most immediate and superficial problem which the student brings up, but to the reality of the community and to the task of becoming an adult. In this way the student may hear a relevant word which is different from the one he came to hear or thought he desired to hear. Teachers who give over to the students the construction of the syllabus and the determination of the teaching material are not being relevant to student needs; they are simply abdicating adult authority and responsibility.

The presentation of Christianity cannot be entirely without structure. If teaching is to continue over any length of time there must be broad guidelines within which a number of different teachers can work. However, on the day-to-day basis that an individual teacher operates, there could be an almost complete absence of visible structure, that is, a movement dictated by no clear lines of logical argumentation, historical sequence, or doctrinal system. This kind of teaching could be much closer to the actual human and Christian reality than any highly organized system could be. I readily admit the need for unity, sequence and organization; but these arise differently on a personal level by ways that logic cannot entirely dictate beforehand. I think that we are still obsessively concerned with saying everything, saying it once, and saying it in the supposed proper arrangement. Religion teachers are still encouraged to say far too many things with far too many words. The Christian faith does not consist in a long list of things all of which must be said at some point lest the student be missing that part of revelation. Christianity is a communion which is a "given" in man's life to be freely accepted. Schools do not give the revelation to the student but they could give the student some help to understand it. Teachers need not worry about saying everything that could be said. We do not have to get students to understand everything; what they really need is to understand *anything* about Christianity. Given the personal and organic character of Christian revelation, they could take it on their own from this point. If schools could only succeed in awakening a spark of intellectual enthusiasm, people might desire to continue their religious education for a lifetime and eventually discover what it means to be a Christian.

The demands of freedom and the nature of revelation imply that a spirit of dialogue will always be present in the teaching of religon. Not in the unending flow of words from the lips of the catechist but in the calm and gentle exchange between persons does God's revelation happen. This does not necessarily mean that one must always use group discussions for the teaching of religion. It does mean that an atmosphere of dialogue is inherent to the catechetical process. A good religion teacher, even if he is lecturing, always conveys the attitude of searching together with his hearers for an understanding of what God is now asking of them. The experienced teacher knows intuitively that any effective teaching involves discovery on the part of the student and the willingness to submit all of the material to questioning. Unfortunately, religion teachers have often been told that discussions and questioning can have only very limited value in the area of religion teaching. It has been said repeatedly that in the teaching of religion the teacher's role is to announce the message and the student's place is to accept it. The inadequacy of the theological notions here is particularly distressing.

God unites to himself man in his freedom and invites man

to open his mind without fear to all truth. It is in human history that God is revealed and there is no other place for the student to discover revelation except as a reality given in his own life. It is given by God and not by teachers; it is discovered and understood by students in communal experience and personal reflection. The students correctly sense that any truth announced by the teacher cannot be the truth that will set them free. At best it can be a pointer in the right direction.

There is certainly a teaching authority in the Church as there is an authority to scripture and an authority to all the truth discovered by human reason. But the authority functions within the dialogue of God and mankind and not from outside of it. The truth that the Church's present and past tradition provides is to free the individual from his own arbitrariness and prompt him to deeper thinking within the community. No pronouncement of scripture or magisterium could end the need for the dialogue of religion teaching which asks what God is now revealing and now demanding of us.

We believe, as Christians, that the highest ideals of human life are shining forth in the human history of Jesus Christ. The understanding of this life must emerge from a total human context. Christ cannot be inserted by pious phrases, he must appear at the summit of humanity. One does not have a Christ-centered teaching because the name and teachings of Christ are constantly used. We do begin to find the revelation in Christ when we accept human freedom as God's great gift and, by a communion that invites the other to leave his ego-centricity, we together grow toward the complete freedom revealed and accomplished in Jesus Christ.

3. From Content to People

OUR first essay sketched a future for catechetics; the second was descriptive of the present. It would seem useful at this point to say a few words in criticism of the recent past. This is the logical order according to the paradox that we find our true past in the present as we face the future. I do not intend to speak with harshness about the catechetical movement of the past few years. However, my remark in the first essay about the passing of the era of "content" demands some further elaboration.

In preface to criticism I should remark that a dissatisfaction with recent catechetical developments seems to many people to be shockingly disloyal or utterly incomprehensible. Their reaction is fairly easy to understand. For a great number of people in catechetical work, there was a memorable moment two, five or ten years ago, when they were liberated from a stifling system of bad theology. Through some great teacher they discovered how simple, meaningful and beautiful Christianity is. It really can be summed up in a few lines of holy scripture. Thus was rediscovered God's simple way of doing it by bible and liturgy. Faced with a choice between the abstractions of the theology manual and the expressive images of the biblical-liturgical approach, how could anyone possibly fail to choose the latter?

The trouble with this choice is the assumption that there are only two options, and that to choose against one is to opt for the other. I have already referred to the revivifying process that has been taking place in theology. Here I would like to take the question from the other side and challenge the assumption that there is *a* biblical-liturgical approach. Those who speak about "the biblical-liturgical approach" almost invariably have a well-defined content in mind. This was clearly the case with the textbooks that flooded the market. Nearly all of them claimed to have the new biblical-liturgical approach; nearly all of them were depressingly the same.

It could be that there are other ways of teaching Christianity in which the bible and the liturgy are less conspicuous but (partly for that very reason) more effective. Our instincts are correct in wishing to have students "respond to the love of God revealed in the plan of salvation." However, the constant repetition of this objective may destroy the possibility of ever reaching it. Saying all the nice new biblical-liturgical phrases might just be the wrong thing to do with an adolescent in urban America.

The catechetical movement over the past one or two decades has been a European import. I suspect that "the new approach" was never bought by the great majority of American teachers. This may be due to stubbornness and ignorance on the part of the American teachers. But it may also be traceable to good sense and to an intuitive realization that the American approach would be different. In trusting to their experience and practicality rather than to the one, rigid pattern proposed to them, American teachers may have been ahead of the movement rather than behind it.

It is practically unavoidable that the European visitor places American catechetics on a European time-scale. Americans are to be encouraged because their European friends have been through this stage of development many years ago. It is not a sign of ingratitude if we reject this time-scale. We shall continue to be indebted to European circles for work in theology and catechetics, but we need not imitate their stages of development. American Catholicism may instead be in a position to take up a role of leadership in the coming era of church education. Certainly, the characteristics of pluralism in unity, empiricism and practicality, freedom with organization, will be those in need in the new era of religious education. Instead of looking now to Europe we might (as Vincent Novak wrote recently from Europe) have more confidence in American style and experimentation.

I am by no means the first to suggest that a new stage in catechetical developments is upon us. Many writers in European and missionary countries have spoken of a "third age" in modern catechetics. I suspect, however, that the upheaval that is to come may be far greater than most catechetical leaders are envisioning. Whereas they are thinking of it as a smoothing out of institutional and programatic details, I believe that the new stage may look more like a reversal of everything they have been trying to do. I think that the development will be in fact consonant with Jungmann's cry for change back in 1936. It will seem to be destructive only because much of recent catechetical effort has been misdirected to "content" rather than to persons and personal understanding.

Susan Sontag could easily have been referring to catechetics when she wrote: "Whatever it may have been in the past, the idea of content is today mainly a hindrance, a nuisance, a subtle or not so subtle philistinism."[1] Admittedly, this is stating the issue a little harshly. The proposal to improve the content of religion teaching was not altogether bad. Perhaps at one stage of things it was the best thing that could have been said and was said. But this statement of the problem too readily gave the impression that there is a certain collection of Catholic things which make up the content of religion teaching. These things could presumably be placed in books and transferred from head to head. The wrong content which we had was to be replaced by the right content which was being prepared for us. It should be possible in a few lectures to tell the teachers what the content is. The teachers would in their turn

1. Quoted in William Lynch, "Counterrevolution in the Movies," *Commonweal* (October 20, 1967), p. 77.

deliver the content to the students. If someone would just tell us what this new content is, everything could settle down again.

To this question of where to find the new content, the answer seemed fairly obvious: in the pages of holy scripture. This content would not be the bible history of the past or the mangled texts of the theology manual, but instead the most up to date exegesis. In using the "word of God" as his text how could a teacher be wrong? He was guaranteed that he had the right content and the right language; all that remained was to set it out in proper order.

The ordering of the content was provided for the teacher. To describe a pattern discernible in the bible there had been coined the somewhat barbarous phrase "salvation history." With amazing speed this phrase became the Catholic catechetical catchword. As a term to designate some insight into scripture, "salvation history" may have some use. It may be noted, however, that at the very time that the word was becoming so popular in catechetics, it was being severely criticized in both Catholic and Protestant theology. Whatever be its usefulness in exegesis or theology, the phrase "salvation history" is inadequate and misleading as an equivalent for the new contents of the new catechetics.

The point is frequently made these days that "salvation history" is not to be understood in a narrow, biblicist way. It is said that the meaning must be broadened and deepened so that the student's whole life will be understood as part of salvation history. I do not know whether the phrase is salvageable by this kind of move. I suspect that it is not. When one is working from a thin base of understanding, persistent attempts at redefinition often make things worse. Trying to extend the concept "salvation history" is liable to tear apart the patchwork. At any rate, it is pointless to argue for or against salvation history. The real issue is whether teachers and teachers of teachers are asking theological questions about this and other frequently used phrases in catechetical writing. Without this theological perspective we will surely end up with a new system that again obscures the gospel.

Christian theologians in recent years have been engaged in the most serious examination of their basic concepts. They have been asking whether or not there are religious or Christian things at all. They are trying to understand how God's revelation-redemption is related to the whole temporal order. In this regard, Küng, Schlette and Rahner suggest that we speak of Israel and the Christian churches as the extraordinary way of salvation. Most men, it would seem, find their way to God outside of this framework. Schlette goes on to say that the history of Israel is not so much the history of salvation as the revelation of a salvation that is everywhere.[2] Israel and the church are the manifestation of God's grace present in all history, poured out upon all men. What the Pannenberg school is forcefully reaffirming in Protestantism is that there is no salvation history other than the history of the world.[3]

The theology implicit in the preceding paragraph constitutes a challenge for religious education. It seems to me that generally speaking catechetics is still engaged in trying to construct a world outside of the real world of existing people. At a time when all the barriers are falling down, it is busily engaged in forming students within a religious world with a carefully arranged pattern of ideas and special words. An intricate set of events is studied from which students are to extract "revealed truths" to be applied to the contemporary world.

When it is found these days that these truths are not appreciated by students, then the teacher is advised to "come down to their level." Pre-catechesis is thus a key word today; unfortunately this usually means a stage of preparing them before teaching the Christian content. This adaptation of "starting

2. See Heinz Robert Schlette, *Towards a Theology of Religions* (New York, 1966), pp. 86–92.
3. See Wolfhart Pannenberg, "Hermeneutics and Universal History," in *History and Hermeneutic,* ed. Robert Funk and Gerhard Ebeling (New York, 1967), p. 122–152.

where people are" is a partial recognition of what is wrong but the proposed solution is inadequate. Tacking on things, either at beginning or end, will not help. This would leave untouched the more fundamental problem, namely, the block of content which is supposedly God's revealed truth. The theological part of my first essay was meant to challenge the very concept of "revealed truth."

Instead of encasing people within a set of answers and practices, religion teaching must start from the facts of our existing situations. The church can no longer be treated as a refuge of defense against a non-Catholic world of error. Today the church's stance must be one of universal ecumenism. The Christian must meet men where they are and search with them in a spirit of free inquiry for the truth that goes beyond any of us. This position neither affirms the rightness of everything happening in the modern world nor denies the claim of the church to a uniqueness before God. Such an ecclesiology, however, calls into question the present catechetical vision. Even in very recent presentation there is still the image of a catechist delivering the answers drawn from biblical-liturgical material.

The young person of today finds himself standing in the midst of a confused world not of his own making. He is subjected to tremendous pressures and is forced to grope for meaning within a welter of experiences. The Christian teacher is one who hopefully can speak the word that will aid a person in his search for some kind of meaning to it all. The word that proves effective may or may not be a biblical word. It may well be a word that is never directly spoken. God's revelation cannot be identified with any words but a word may help in a man's understanding and acceptance of God's revelation. We do not lower ourselves temporarily to where people are; rather, we start and end with people because that is where God is.

If the large body of content that we think students should

know is hopelessly removed from their lives, perhaps we should reconsider whether this really is the right content. The lack of success in teaching this content may be due to something else besides the deficiencies of students or teachers. Furthermore, the answer to this difficulty is not necessarily found in adapting the content to the students. Before cutting down the content or adding a stage preparatory to it, we should analyze more thoroughly the meaning of content.

The word "content" is very ambiguous in this present context. There is one sense in which all teaching involves a content: things said, experience planned, ideas exchanged. If content means the materials and experiences that can be instrumental in the teaching process, then we have too little content in religion teaching. We have narrowed our sights into one small body of materials. In the hands of a competent teacher all kinds of surprising things might find their way into the content of religion teaching. With this sense of the word, the whole world can be the content and we have hardly begun to touch the possibilities.

Content has a second meaning, however, that usually functions when the word is left unexamined. It is assumed that there is a body of materials that is the content of Christian faith, and that the teacher's role is to convince people to accept this content as true. These days the content consists of a large, technical collection of exegetical, historical and theological materials. In this sense of the word "content" we have far too much of it. I mean not only that the religion curriculums of elementary and secondary schools are impossibly and absurdly large. I mean much more basically that at no level of education is there a specific and definable content that is the religion course. Every truth reveals God even though the Christian believes that some persons and experiences are more revelatory than others.

The denial of any set content to religion teaching could be interpreted as an assault upon the bible and the liturgy. Some people may think that I am trying to reduce the importance of the bible and liturgy for religious education. This is not my intention at all. I think that the bible and liturgy are supremely important for Christian teaching, but I also think that little good is done by wielding them as artificial instruments. Instead of showing us the way to approach our task, the bible and liturgy are being used as the new content. The result is that we overlook the most important contribution that the bible and liturgy could make.

Holy scripture, used as the source of the new content, will inevitably become a rigidly systematized body of data. This will happen because scripture cannot be true to itself unless it points beyond itself. When used as the main subject matter in religion teaching, it becomes an end in itself. It becomes the truths to be known rather than the pointer to what is going on. The wildly exuberant biblical writings get hacked into shape to fit the system.

Scripture is prayer and it is art. It is the church's most beautiful expression of faith and the fecundating principle of all teaching. It is imaginative stories to delight little children and profound insights for mature adults. But holy scripture is not something to grind through again and again in every school year. It is not the pattern on which all textbooks and syllabuses are to be constructed.

Holy scripture is a high point in the inspiring religious literature of men. A high point by definition requires lesser points along the way. Religion teaching must include a wide and rich variety of other writings and experiences. It is no denigration of the bible to suggest that the scriptural literature should play a less obvious, more indirect role in most stages of religious education. Langdon Gilkey has pointed out that it is precisely in those sects where the bible is to be taken "straight" that the bible is unintelligible, incredible and not known. In our culture, Gilkey concludes, the bible will be appreciated only through the mediation of theological learning.[4] Unless a more relaxed, organic and unostentatious use is made of scripture in the teaching situation, a very bad reaction is going to set in. We will not have the help of scripture in understanding the realities it points to and expresses.

Similar but worse difficulties arise when the liturgy is made the source of content for religion classes. Liturgy is badly used today because it is being *used*. Liturgy is not things to be used in teaching; it is prayer. If we let the liturgy be itself, it might teach us not to concentrate so grimly on saying all the right things that supposedly need saying. What we could learn from the liturgy is that truth must emerge out of reverence, artistry, dialogue, play and silence.

Anyone who sets out to teach Christian faith must be filled with the spirit that the liturgy is to breathe. How many liturgical sounding things he says is quite another matter. Most of the current attempts to drag the liturgy into religion teaching are even more artificial than the uses made of scripture. We need not so much a teaching of liturgy as a teaching of foundational materials that might eventually find expression within a liturgical act. Otherwise, we are soon to have an anti-liturgical movement. This would be tragic if a reaction set in against the liturgy before we have hardly begun to explore what the liturgy is supposed to mean for us today. No help at all will be forthcoming from the self-conscious, obsessional kind of approach inevitable when the liturgy is the content of religion courses.

My criticism may seem to be shaking the carefully built improvements of recent years. I do not wish to be negative or destructive, and I certainly do not wish to turn back the clock. I wish only to get beyond the globs of undigested material that stand in the way.

It is legitimate to demand of a critic that if he does not like

4. *How the Church Can Minister to the World Without Losing Itself* (New York, 1964), p. 97.

what is being done, then he should propose an alternative that is better. But it is wrong to demand that it be the same *kind* of alternative. People who think in the categories of objects, systems and contents tend to think that the only alternatives are other objects, systems and contents. But there is a different kind of change at work in the church today: the giving of priority to persons over any pre-formed system. For example, the alternative to a Catholic school is not necessarily a CCD school, it might be a team of people who would do whatever is helpful for education in a concrete situation. Many administrators find such proposals too vague and indefinite; but the proposal is not vague. It is quite clear and explicit what is being proposed; the unknown factor is what the results will be. The one main question is whether there is a trust of the people.

My alternative, therefore, is not to replace the things we are doing with other things. Textbooks and syllabuses may need changing but the change will probably not help much. Staking our hopes on this kind of change may lead to increased frustrations. We have to begin by realizing the limitations inherent even in the best of textbooks. This in itself would be a great liberation. What needs changing is the attitude toward textbooks. With this happening, teachers would have the confidence and understanding to adapt, synthesize and omit materials in an intelligent way. Whatever is the case in other fields, in religion a good teacher is a little helped by a good text and not obstructed by a bad text; a poor teacher is probably made worse by a poor text and usually confused by a good text.

Theological questioning on the part of the teacher is the only real means of advance. In proposing this I do not wish to destroy people's confidence or discourage them in what they are now doing. I am aware that discouragement or despair may be a side-effect of this questioning. But if we really begin to think of the person as the center of the catechetical process, teachers would be encouraged to look for their own answers by reading, reflection, discussion and experimentation. They

66

would give up their expectation of a perfected, new content descending from on high. At the same time, because they could act with confidence on the basis of their own experience, they would have a firmer ground for their hope.

Theological inquiry as the center of all teacher preparation may sound very unrealistic. It is difficult enough to give simple courses of instruction to tens of thousands of catechists. Can one seriously propose to move beyond the simplicity of scripture to deeply theological concerns? The answer I have earlier indicated is that for an adult community today scripture will remain simple only within a theologizing context. The trouble with teacher-training courses that try to deliver the new content is not that they are too simple but that they are too complex.

The same misake is being made with teachers as was once made in preparing confessors. Instead of trusting in intelligence there is an attempt to supply all the answers before the process begins. At first it looks like a simpler, easier, surer way to prepare people. Eventually, however, as the holes of the pattern fill in, the result is a horrible and deadening mass of detail. Wherever people are not trusted to use their own intelligence, then complications develop. If there are teachers who are incapable of using their minds in this way, this would seem to be the sure proof that they should not be teaching at all. Giving these teachers courses in content and method merely hides the real problem and perpetuates a system that may not only be useless but harmful.

Teacher training would therefore be largely a matter of theologizing. Or, to put all of this in proper order, the main work of religious education would be providing this kind of theology for the adults in the church. Some of those adults might in turn teach other adults or young people. The actual content of these courses will be discovered as the person who has theologized meets the community of people whom he is to teach.

This approach to religious education would make greater

demands upon people but it is in many ways a simpler process. Good Christian theology at its most theoretical and speculative rejoins the simple Christian life in the flesh. This is so because, unlike gnosticism that promises salvation only to those few who can grasp the secrets of the gods, Christianity maintains that the Word has become flesh. A developed Christian theology always comes back to flesh, to the person in wholeness and simplicity. As Rahner has often said, it is the bad, half-done theology that gets into impossible complications which the ordinary person finds unintelligible.[5] Catechetics is in danger of being overburdened once more with the technicalities it sought to escape from. To achieve a new simplicity we need the kind of theological vision that presses beyond the complexity of contents and reintegrates all of this into the unity of the person.

5. See Karl Rahner, *The Christian Commitment* (New York, 1963), p. 103.

4. No Half Revolutions

IN THE brilliant motion picture, *The Battle of Algiers,* there is portrayed the struggle of a few rebels to carry through a liberation movement. At one point the rebel leader says: "To start a revolution is difficult; to sustain it is more difficult; to win it is more difficult still. But when you have won it, then your troubles really begin." Despite the rapid changes taking place in religious education, I do not think that our troubles have really begun.

We are on the verge of a great new breakthrough in the field of religious education. There is no guarantee, however, that this advance will take place. Unless there is continuing self-criticism the catechetical movement is liable to suffocate itself. There will be newer and more attractive textbooks, more and more mysterious catechetical language, bigger and better national conferences; but the opportunity will have passed. In this essay I wish to continue the theme of the person as center of the revolution and ask what this means in regard to teachers and students.

There surely have been worse times than the present for religious education. Those who have been at this work for a much longer time than I have, could testify to this fact. It may seem inappropriate to be critical just when things are finally beginning to happen. But the problem of modern times—a problem that goes beyond religion teaching or schools—is not that we have too few revolutions nor that we have too many revolutions, but that we have so many half-revolutions. There is nothing so stale, nothing that weighs so heavily upon human life and progress as a half-perfected revolution.

At the beginning of a revolution we are sure of what we are against; we also know that we have discovered something exciting and new. We use all of our energies to escape from the old confining system. At last, we manage to free ourselves by destroying the old system or beating it into helpless submission. But while we are congratulating ourselves for this escape we may fail to recognize that we are now in a new system, that is, a self-enclosed set of answers to a predetermined set of questions. We are amazed that everyone else is not so excited about the new revolutionary things. We do not notice that we have already begun to cake it all in a new esoteric language. Instead of criticising our new ideas we try simply to defend and to implement them. Thus we settle for something less than real revolution.

My own judgment about the catechetical movement is that it is half-way to a revolution. This is not meant to be a condemnation. One could hardly expect it to be any further. Half-way represents a great amount of progress. My fear, however, is that many people are mistaking these first steps for the whole revolution. We have spawned enough knowledge to get a revolution going; do we have enough not merely to keep it in existence but to accelerate it—which is the only way to carry through a revolution? We have just about knocked dead the traditional catechism but it may be that we are replacing it with a new and stifling system which is closed in on itself. We might not notice this for several years because the introduction of anything new into religion classes will be welcomed by students. But what happens when the high school student says: "Not those events of salvation history again; why can't we have something new for a change?"

More specifically, I would say that the introduction of the new content, which I spoke of in the last essay, has been a great gain but that it is not the revolution. The widespread assumption that it is the use of scriptural and liturgical material that will improve religion teaching is not quite accurate; at best such a program is incomplete. Religious education in

70

which children are inserted into a tradition is inadequate for our age. The Baltimore Catechism was poor preparation for living in the middle ages. Much recent catechetical material is good preparation—for living in the middle ages. But fortunately or unfortunately the middle ages do not exist. My remark is not meant simply as sarcasm. I am referring to the precise difference between medieval and modern periods, namely, the emergence of the individual, critical intelligence that challenges tradition as such. As Pannenberg has insisted, the issue since the time of the Enlightenment has been the authority of any kind of revelation.[1] Perfecting the biblical-liturgical context as our textbooks do and attempting to place children within that structure may not be what we need at all. I am not saying that I could write a better textbook than those now being written. I am glad that someone is writing better books than we had. But the paraphernalia of which the religion textbook is the epitome is centuries out of touch with students in 1968.

I would like to reiterate my attitude toward the scriptural and liturgical movements. I think that teachers need to understand scripture and appreciate the liturgy. Far from wishing to lessen their role in religious education I would like to see more scripture and liturgy used with young children. I would like to see them soaked in it because there are some things which must be gotten at that time of life or it will be a near impossibility to get them later. The point I wish to stress, however, is that we must not stop there. Teachers should not aim to acquire a knowledge of scripture and liturgy but an integrated theological understanding. Any theology that is worth anything today will take into itself the scriptural and liturgical, but it will also involve critical human reflection upon the symbols that are specifically Christian.

You may object to this demand for theology because you teach in the first grade and you do not intend to teach your students any theology. That is fine; I agree entirely. But I

1. See his "Response to the Discussion," in *Theology as History*, ed. James M. Robinson and John B. Cobb (New York, 1967), pp. 229–30.

maintain that the only way you will avoid teaching them a lot of bad theology is to know some good theology. The teacher who understands theology will know that his task is not to use the latest words and ideas of the theologians but to introduce the children to the reality of Christian faith by a variety of images and experiences.

Teachers who refuse to wrestle with theology and who think that they are escaping theology end up by teaching the most theology in the most theologically laden language. These days we have Rahner and Schillebeeckx being taught in the third grade and this I find disastrous. But there is no way to avoid it except by studying Rahner, Schillebeeckx or other good theologians. If parents and teachers of the young study theology they will not find out what to say to children, but they might find out a lot of things that they should not say, and that certainly would be an improvement.

In the schools one cannot examine Christian life without stirring up questions which are in the broad sense theological. To think that this can be avoided is the surest way to introduce bad theology. It is a fallacy to suppose that the lower the level of instruction, the less the theological preparation needed. It might be better to put the most theologically competent people with the small children. One can almost get along without teachers in a graduate school; those students can always go to the library. But small children are at the mercy of an adult world which assumes that anything is good enough for children. A child in the first grade needs a teacher, that is, someone who knows Catholic theology and knows how to teach small children.

It may seem idealistic to propose that parents and teachers study theology; idealistic it is but a possibility nonetheless. Most intelligent people are quite capable of handling the subject when they put their minds to it. The real trouble is that one finds, especially among 30 and 40-year-old priests and religious, a slight tremor at the word "theology." Theology means for some of these people the suffocating thing hammered into them in required courses. They are perhaps unaware of what has been happening in theology. Once people get a good taste of it they find it not at all uninteresting and not really so confusing.

Competent religion teachers can usually be gotten only with competent training. Religious orders that run schools are still not quite ready to admit this fact. With some subtle persuasion a sister can get to a summer workshop or institute. What she really needs is one or several years so that she can feel at home in the field. Not everyone can be provided with such opportunities, but advanced study for some would improve the quality of work at every level. The improvement at first will be slow, perhaps imperceptible. The one question worth asking, however, is whether we plan eventually to do the job in the right way. We can keep putting patches on things as we are now generally doing, or else we can resolutely begin to prepare for an adequate program in the future. By the future I do not mean the next century; I mean five to ten years from now.

The tactical move here is crystal clear: commit a good number of people to full-time study. In a year or two there would already be a corps of people around which to build. Dioceses are not doing this though the cost would be minute compared to the total cost of the educational institutions. Religious orders are not doing it because of the exodus from religious life. One can sympathize with the tremendous problem all of this entails for religious superiors. Nevertheless, preparing their people to be theologically competent is in the long run the way that religious orders have some chance to survive.

It is true that there are not many programs of study available in this country. One of the main reasons for the lack of supply is that up until recently there was almost no demand. If all the religious orders suddenly decided to take up this work in earnestness there would be an oversaturation of existing facilities. This would in time balance off or else the pressure of the orders' demand would force the issue of a more rational plan for using the resources we do have in the country. Here is where the religious orders could make a real contribution to the laity. The religious education will eventually be controlled by laity but the individual layman is almost powerless to effect the reinstitutionalization needed.

I will not try to answer the question of whether all or only some of the members of religious teaching communities should teach religion. If religious orders put their minds to it they could get most of their people to a level where they could make a solid contribution to religious education. Whether this would be in the formal way of classroom teaching is a separate question. As I have outlined in my introductory essay, religious education is not co-extensive with either Catholic schools or "Catholic education." The religious orders should be exploring the different possibilities for religious education that would draw on all the talents of their religious men and women.

I shift my focus of concern at this point from the teacher to the student. The student of today is growing up in a world that is quite different from apostolic times, middle ages, a century ago or a generation ago. In an age of religious tradition it is possible to form children within the tradition and be fairly confident that they will stay there and that they will see the world from that perspective. This kind of world does not exist today. Students in our culture are exposed to an immense variety of ideas, experiences, attitudes and activities.

The question of children today is not how to be formed by their teachers and how to observe the precepts of their tradition. Their question today, and it is a question they are forced to ask today, is: How do I become free? Their search is for that which is more human and for that direction in which lies the fullness of truth. In catechetical literature there is regular reference to freedom, the freedom of the sons of God. There is, however, practically no realization of the delicate and paradoxical position of the catechist vis-à-vis human freedom. To our announced programs for the formation of their freedom, the answer of an increasing number of students is: No thanks; we prefer to do this for ourselves.

74

You may think that this is a terrible state of affairs and that the world will destroy itself if it keeps going this way. That may indeed be so. The one thing certain, however, is that there is no way back. The one thing that modern man can never again do is submit unreflexively to nature. Consciousness has been opened out; freedom has become central and can never again be peripheral. The question for theologians and religious educators is not whether to accept this fact but how to understand the given fact relative to Christian faith. They must examine whether Christianity is being edged out of the world or whether it is for the first time finding its proper milieu. In either case, something world-shaking is occurring and our understanding or lack of understanding of the process will determine our approach to religious education.

Christianity, I would suggest, is being pressured more than ever before into realizing its true and proper mission. This mission consists not in suppressing some part of the world or some human goods in favor of others. It is the affirming of all human values and the taking up of all that is human to push the human beyond itself. What Christianity could offer today is the incentive to open understanding and freedom to the boundless reality of personal value and communal love.

The Christian believes that the relationship to God as revealed in Jesus Christ and his church is the gateway to the expansion of freedom and love. Often in the past, especially when the situation was exacerbated by post-reformational struggles, we have based Christianity upon negation. We have attempted to insert God into the world at that point where the human broke down. The clear call to us today is to find God through accepting all that is human. God will thus be found not as a piece of this world but as its presupposition and end. No religious tradition that closes in on itself and tries to ward off the growth of freedom and intelligence has a possibility of survival in today's world.

If such a theological vision were operative in the church,

there would be repercussions at every stage of student development. In the first place, the young child's relation to his parents would be seen as crucial to the process of religious education. Parents would understand that their role consists in the provision of an experience of Christian adulthood. Thus, the child would have a model with which to understand that Christianity is a religion lived by grown ups. Religious education for little children would not be confused with teaching them cute little prayers and pious practices. These may be not only useless but an obstacle to the growth of their grace-filled lives. With small children today it is time to give an opportunity to the human spirit and to the Holy Spirit. The indispensable contribution of parents to the religious training of their children is the breaking down of fear by the giving of love.

At school age there is a time for letting children experience and absorb the universal human symbols that Christianity has incorporated. The focus ought to be the experience itself. One need not draw out everything from a biblical story; one hardly need draw out anything at all. Why do anything to a good story if the child thinks it is a good story? In appreciating the narrative as revelatory the child is more perceptive than many adults who are looking for revealed truths contained in the bible.

Liturgical experience can be very simple. Certainly, it should rely primarily upon the child's own experienced world. If the liturgy is ever to be renewed it will have to be through teachers meeting children in attentiveness to the wide range of joys and sorrows in human life. Out of a sensivity to all the beauties and marvels of nature and history there may some day arise in a future generation a real celebration of God and creation. Teachers do not have to give this sensitivity to children. They just have to find the ways to prevent this sensitivity from being snuffed out in a child's life.

I am only too well aware that this kind of teaching requires skilled and patient teachers. We do not have enough of these teachers and probably never will. This makes it the more imperative that the good teachers we do have be given free rein to treat little children like little children. Some excellent teachers who do know what little children are like have often been hampered by external authorities who are interested in results. By results they mean the twelve articles of the creed, the ten commandments and innumerable other things that little children should not be taught. There is no easy solution for this problem though I am optimistic that there has been much progress of late. All that I can suggest to those who exercise authority in these matters is: (1) to learn more about the personal character of Christian revelation which exists in fullness in little children despite their inability to cite the Council of Constantinople; (2) to trust their competent teachers who know little children.

The next stage of the process is the one most in need of critical examination. Little children, I have said, should be allowed to absorb the simple, symbolic activities of Christian tradition. The reason for this assimilation is not that they should close in on this sector of reality but that they will thereby be opened out to all reality. In genuine love there is a necessary moment of exclusivity which is part of a larger movement of inclusivity that is all-embracing. The movement outward in religious thinking cannot be hindered or delayed. In his essay on Christian education, Paul Tillich has stated this idea well: "Very early the humanistic problem makes itself felt. As long as the pupil lives in a dreaming innocence of critical questions, he should not be awakened. But our time is not favorable for a long preservation of such innocence. And if the first critical questions are asked by the child, the first cautious answers must be given. Later on, the questions will become more critical, and the answers must become bolder and more fundamental."[2]

2. "A Theology of Education," in *Theology and Culture* (New York, 1964), p. 156.

This means that one cannot hope so to form people in a scriptural-liturgical framework that they will ask no critical questions beyond that framework. Even if one could manage to do such a thing it would not be advisable today. Neither is it advisable today to put off critical questions which can only be met through the application of human intelligence. Schools of their very nature are supposed to stir up such questioning. Far from resisting this questioning in religion teaching, we ought to welcome it. Christian revelation takes into itself man's reason; and the more that human understanding is released for its proper work, the better for Christian faith.

The questions arise early because our society and our schools impel the student to raise the questions. Early in his schooling he will ask: What is the relation between these "Catholic things" being given to me and the whole universe of truth and freedom? The child may not articulate it in those words but he is most certainly asking the question. When he begins to ask it there had better be someone in the vicinity with enough theological understanding to give the child an intelligent answer.

I would strongly suspect, though I do not know whether the scientific evidence is conclusive, that children today are attaining this critical use of intelligence earlier than ever. That this does not always show up in the school does not disprove the thesis. We have so little realization of all the factors that have recently come into play in education. Television, as the most obvious but only one influence, is itself revolutionary in the upbringing of children. What is primary here is not what they have learned but the novel ways of learning, the swirling vortex of involvement, and the ineluctable pressures to question everything.

If today's teacher hopes to give intelligent answers to the questions of children, he will have had to reflect on his own faith. Of course, it is easy just to stop the child, even easier brutally to overcome him or laugh at him. Children treated this way soon come to understand that they should not address intelligent questions to adults, least of all religion teachers.

Some of the teachers doing their best to stir up enthusiasm in senior high school are finding that they are about ten years too late. We do not need more theological explanations in the third grade; perhaps we should not have religion courses at all in the third grade. But we do need teachers who will not stifle the inquiring minds of third-graders.

I do not mean to concentrate all my attack upon elementary school teachers. There is a universal tendency to pass the buck and blame the previous teachers. It is a fact, nonetheless, that what can be done on high school and college levels depends very much on how the questions were answered by the earliest teachers. Many parents discover too late that they cannot give any sex instruction to their child because they evaded the question or lied to the child when the issue was first raised. Five years olds do not need a course on the physiology of reproductive organs. They do need someone to give them a truthful and respectful answer to their particular questions. Whether or not children are given religion courses they will ask religious questions. They should be answered with the truth as far as we understand it and in terms they will understand. They should not be fed with evasions and downright falsehoods. There is a place for serious intellectual inquiry in Christianity that will not take place in college unless it has its beginnings in the grade school.

Men of this generation are still impressed by the organization and complexity of the church, the breadth and beauty of her activities. But many of these same people believe that the church really has nothing to say; serious questions are not allowed. The only sufficient answer to this charge is to begin asking such questions. If teachers would believe in their own work and get on with the task of teaching, they could contribute in a small way to making Christianity alive. Despite my critical remarks here I think that we have come a long way. All I can urge is: On with the revolution.

5. Catechism Come of Age

THE MOST amazing thing about the *New Catechism* from Holland is not that it has been done well but that it has been done at all. I hasten to add that it is indeed a well-done book. Whatever defects reviewers, users or ecclesiastical investigators may find, the Dutch Catechism is a decisive step into the future. Those who heard ten years ago that the German Catechism was the last word may be distrustful of great enthusiasm at this point. There may be some problems of adaptation with this book but it represents a far bolder step than the German Catechism or those that followed immediately in its wake.

The distinctive thing about this catechism is that it is a book for adults. This is not entirely unique inasmuch as the catechism which issued from the Council of Trent was also for adults. But the particular turn that the catechism took in the following centuries has made the word synonymous with the sing-song tale of a child. Whether or not the word "catechism" can be recovered from this graveyard is debatable. But if there is a future at all to the catechism it seems certain that it will have to be of the kind that this book is.

Some people in this country will no doubt be bothered by the theology that is found in this book. It is to be hoped that they are bothered enough to read the book thoroughly and consider the theology carefully. There is no denying that the book has the stamp of the progressive Dutch theologians. This is not to say that it is a book of extreme positions. In very large part, it is simply descriptive and factual, devoid of abstract theorizing and sweeping judgments. As a matter of fact, it is most striking in what it does not say.

A reviewer can only dip into a little of the contents and make some comments on points that have attracted widespread attention. A few prefatory remarks must be made, however, on the methodology of the whole work. The introduction informs us that this it not a book at all but a library of books from which the reader can choose. One can start where he likes and read as much as he wishes. But it is a little difficult to reconcile this principle with another statement of the introduction to the effect that many things in the book can be taken as true only within a large enough context. In any case, if this is a small library, the books are certainly placed in a way that tries to make the library a consistent whole.

The catechism, like the gospel it tries to restate, is addressed to the whole world. For this purpose the writers searched for a simple language that would not require of readers a technical theological training. The book does not assume a body of Christian truths that are to be applied to the world. Its methodology is the reverse. The procedure is to take the questions of the contemporary world and ask how the gospel might throw light upon them. The presupposition in this movement from experienced reality to formulated gospel is the book's claim that the bible is not a pious book but an "echo of reality."

This concern to proceed from the real questions of real people is convincingly shown in the first twenty pages of the book. One might wish that this section on "Man the Questioner" were longer, but that it is there at all as the beginning of a catechism is a great accomplishment. By examples of both happiness and suffering, a quest for some kind of ultimate meaning is revealed. But instead of concluding that there is a God whom we know by reason, the catechism brings in the fact of Christian faith as a challenge. Then in a final twist the section ends with the counter-challenge of evil.

In the following parts of the catechism the general outline is historical although not narrowly chronological. There are clear and positive summaries of other religions; one of these

81

is of Marxism, which is described as a pre-Christian religion. Judaism and Christianity are presented as unique expressions of God's revelation but with parallels in the life of each individual and humanity as a whole. The secularity motif runs throughout discussions of revelation and redemption. God is at work in the whole of creation and man is never fully able to grasp the process. Christianity has influenced other religions and secular humanism as well, while at the same time Christianity has discovered something of its own self in these encounters.

The long section on the gospels is less interesting to read only because it includes the kind of compressed factual detail one would expect in a book like this. Occasionally, one is struck by sentences that reveal a quite different approach in christology. Of Jesus' human consciousness, we read: "The world dawned on him as on any other human being." The 12-year-old Christ in the temple is described thus: "An intelligent boy discovers his vocation." The miracles are characterized not so much as spectacular feats but as "something unexpectedly mild and gracious." Concerning the infancy narratives and particularly the virgin birth, there is nothing denied; there is also not a great deal affirmed beyond saying that Jesus was *the* gift of God, the answer to the prayer of a whole people.

There is a strong emphasis in the scriptural part and also later in the book on the value of prayer. Jesus' direct communion with his Father was in the moments withdrawn for prayer. The liturgical year and a description of liturgical rites are interwoven through the scripture and the remaining parts of the book. The descriptions can only be of limited value inasmuch as the rites themselves are undergoing such radical change.

The historical theme is carried through to include Christian times but with extreme brevity. One of the constant concerns in narrating church history is the danger of uniting church and secular authority. The separation of church and state is handled in a full chapter toward the end of the book. The reformers revealed by history are dealt with in kind and positive ways. There is also constant pointing to the future where the new knowledge, leisure and arts are to be the chief concern of the church.

The catechism retains much of the traditional schematization of moral and sacramental life, for example the division of faith, hope and charity. Sin plays a decidedly secondary role in the catechism. It shows up for formal treatment about half-way through the book. Here we find the "sin of the world" thesis with which Dutch theologians have been broadening the traditional original-sin concept. Personal sin has little explicit treatment until the last section of the book.

Difficulties of faith are described in detail and with sympathy. Although the catechism sees a value to "social faith" that a person receives in belonging to a Catholic family, it strongly asserts the need for an adult decision to make faith one's own. It even indicates that some people might do better to leave the faith, at least for a while. In this connection, it suggests that the willingness of the adult to let the young person make such a choice is more a test for the adult than for the adolescent.

The treatment of the Eucharist will no doubt be surprising to some people. The liturgical celebration is the central focus. This procedure is well established today in sacramental writing, but the catechism establishes its priorities with such insistence that the real presence of Christ in the eucharistic species is dealt with almost as an afterthought. Christ's presence is, of course, affirmed but without some of the technical apparatus that has been standard in Catholic works. With the sacrament of penance there is no great imagination or novelty. This probably reflects the somewhat desperate plight of this liturgical act in the contemporary church.

The section on marriage stands in sharp contrast to the standard treatises dominated by canon law. The attempt here is to be descriptive of what constitutes love and marriage. There is disapproval of homosexuality and pre-marital intercourse but no harsh judgments. The indissolubility of Christian marriage is supported with the caution that we are not always sure when in fact such a marriage exists. Where a person's conscience conflicts with the church's law on the validity of a marriage, he is not told simply to bear up with the law; he is challenged rather to find the answer he can live with in his own life. Particularly on the question of birth control there are some understanding words for what has been the church's stand. But in the last analysis the choice of means for responsible parenthood is a matter not for doctor or priest but for a person's conscience.

The extremely brief treatment of the celibate's vocation reflects how thinking on marriage has quickly outstripped theological development on the religious life. This section is not without some fine phrases but a theology of the life or even a good description of it seems lacking. The treatment of religious obedience, for example, is totally inadequate. There is also hardly a hint that the question of celibacy is inseparable from the question of community.

The last section of the catechism deals expectedly enough with "last things"; somewhat surprisingly it also treats of God. Not that one does not expect to find God in any section of a catechism; one is just caught short in realizing that not too much has been said of a doctrine of God up to this point. It is obviously implied throughout the book but a formulation of the Trinity is reserved to the end. As for last things, hell still finds a place, a fact that will no doubt please some people. Some kind of hell remains a possibility although children should not be motivated by the threat of it.

We have, therefore, a one-volume summary of Catholic faith which ends with a God always inviting us to open our minds further and create a new future. Christian doctrine in this book functions as the "negation of human negation," the impulse to carry forward the struggle against evil, ignorance and human failure. God, in some obscure way, is the one who is struggling with us.

84

6. Crises of Faith

CHRISTIAN faith has always presented some difficulty for those in the process of growing up. In the past, however, the question generally posed by the teacher of the young was how to find and make use of the right tools for getting the youngster over this difficult period. This conception of the problem is no longer tenable. A more radical and searching examination of the meaning of faith itself is what is called for today. In this essay I shall deal first with the contemporary world's difficulties with faith, second, with the proper Christian response to these difficulties; third, with the peculiar character of the adolescent faith crisis.

We are today in a period of great crisis in regard to Christian faith. That statement is so commonplace these days that it is almost a platitude. Perhaps it is platitudinous since Christian faith always has been and presumbaly always will be in a state of crisis. Whether this crisis is really worse today is I think highly debatable. One need not maintain that the world is getting better and better every day in every way to hold that at the very least contemporary developments are religiously ambivalent. No era of Christianity can make a final judgment on its own worth, and perhaps the safest thing—or the only thing —we can say is that no judgment should be made, because the issue still hangs in the balance.

To say that every era of faith has had its problems is not to deny all novelty to our present situation. It is only in the modern era that the question of faith has itself become thematized for theological inquiry. The question of faith had previously lain beneath the surface as a continuing undercurrent to theological and religious discussions. But as many other religious issues have evaporated and as a multiplicity of distracting questions has been recognized as merely distractive, the central problem of faith has emerged into conscious and reflexive clarity. The contemporary world's difficulties with Christian faith might be characterized by the three terms of apathy, absence and attack.

The first attitude, that of apathy, has always been with us and perhaps needs no examination or explanation. The one question that may need asking is whether apathy is particularly striking or widespread in our day. In many respects it would seem easier to be apathetic in a world which provides a luxuriance of pleasant diversions. Much of American advertising, for example, seems dedicated to the obscuration of life's harsh realities and the destruction of all deep probing into the ultimate mysteries of life.

On the other hand, there are characteristics of our contemporary world that seem to make apathy less of a possibility. In particular there seems to be more recognition of the precariousness of human existence and the need for responsible decisions. There is a new seriousness in the sixties often accompanied by great pessimism about the world and its future. The theme of many of the folk songs being sung by young people today is not "when I grow up . . . ," but "if by any chance I should grow up . . ." In a world faced daily with decisions of peace, justice and survival, apathy or indifference regarding faith hardly seems to be the appropriate response.

It is somewhat surprising, therefore, that the constant complaint of college teachers of theology is the apathy of the students. This is a frustrating situation to be sure, and we are liable to feel that it is useless to go any further. What is the sense of discussing a lot of historical and theological data when the problem is that the listeners have no interest in any of it? I am not sure that I have the answer to that question but I suggest that it is through understanding the other reactions and their causes that we might best come to grips with the problem of apathy. For many people apathy is not indifference; it is a definite answer to questions which they recognize as not at all unimportant. They have decided (sometimes while retaining all the right practices) that Christian faith is not to be taken seriously. This conviction is not always the fault of the man currently trying to preach or teach the faith. Apathy is born of years of listening to tired preachers preaching meaningless answers to unintelligible questions. Rather than let this reaction of apathy paralyze our efforts, I am suggesting that we look at the other attitudes which though characterizing the minority may hold the key to understanding the majority.

I have named the second reaction absence, that is, the experience of emptiness, loneliness and abandonment. This is a phenomenon peculiar to our own day. Whatever problems men of the ancient world may have had, they never had a lack of gods. Primitive religions oscillated between monotheism and polytheism; gods died and were reborn. With the advance of Western civilization, however, the heavens were stripped of the gods until only the Judaic-Christian God could make serious claim to man's allegiance. But now he too seems eclipsed behind the heavens. Nietzsche's flamboyant and paradoxical announcement of the death of God seemed until recently to be of small significance. But now the word is out (mostly via *Time* magazine) that the radical left of Christian theologians is wrestling with this utter absence of God as the starting point of Christian faith. One may have reservations about these new and suddenly famous theologians. I think, nevertheless, that they are witnessing to an experience more common in contemporary life than we have usually admitted, namely, the feeling that God is absent from the world, the conclusion that there are no longer any "religious questions" which belong to a special province of supernatural faith, the uneasy but inescapable conviction that religious beliefs, practices and devotions are embarrassingly naïve.

87

The evolution of this predicament of God being edged out of the world is fairly easy to trace at least on a visible level. For centuries Christian apologetics kept just one step ahead of an advancing science that was giving better answers than religion could. A place was always found for God but he became the God of the interstices, the one who filled the gaps in scientific explanations. Scientific progress, however, has meant a steady retreat of faith from each position successively taken up. In the long course of its historical development, science is no closer today than it was in the past of disproving God; but undeniably it has made man feel less and less the need for God. He died by inches, by the successive qualifications, by the ridiculous-looking rear-guard action fought in his name. This process has become apparent only in the past few decades with the acceleration of scientific and technological progress, but the fact of this process is an inescapable feature of our present world. When I say inescapable, I am carefully choosing the word. The air we breathe is that of a scientific world and no man can simply escape from this world to construct his own set of beliefs unaffected by modern scientific criticism.

Scientific technology, then, has been the most obvious factor in the developing crisis of Christian faith. I think, however, that it is not the most profound cause. The most important key to the understanding of the contemporary faith problem is found in the third attitude, that which I have called attack. By attack I do not mean here the kind of opposition that has been common in the history of Christianity. There have always been those who rejected Christian faith because they preferred self-interests or a more rational explanation, or an easier code of life. But the attack upon Christian faith peculiar to the present is based upon the charge that Christianity is just not good enough, that it degrades man, that it is lacking in charity. Those who see Christianity this way base their contention upon both the theoretical works of Christian writers and the practical consequences that have resulted. Camus was led to conclude that only an atheist could truly be charitable.

The issue in the minds of these men is to choose between God and man. Faced with such a choice there can be little doubt what the outcome must be. And so it has happened in the last century that men have passionately defended humanity against the avenging and destructive God of Christian faith. "Life is destroyed by the beyond," wrote Feuerbach, "the disintegrating, poisoning, bloodsucking—why a beyond if not as a means for besmirching this world. The concept of God was constructed as a contradiction to life—it contains everything harmful, defaming, everything at enmity with life." Philosophy, I would strongly suspect, could never of itself have given birth to such agonizing and demonic cries. It was rather out of a desperate struggle against a corrupted notion of Christian faith that this violent attack upon God arose.

The most profound difficulty we face is not the advance of science but the fact that Christian faith has *never* been able to present a united front to rethink its position vis-à-vis this scientific world. Modern science arose in a world torn by an internecine war of Christian faith. In the Reformation struggle and its resulting oppositions a partial negation of human values was incorporated into Protestant and Catholic conceptions of faith. So long as faith is justified on such a basis there is little hope for a real coming to grips with the whole human problem of faith. The reformational and post-reformational struggles instead of healing the split between faith and reason exacerbated the situation, opposing the more strongly faith and reason, the this-worldly and the other-worldly, the nearness of God and his transcendence above the heavens.

That is why the ecumenical movement is not a peripheral question here. The Christian response to the contemporary crisis of faith is inextricably bound up with the unresolved problems within Christian faith. What is called for today in answer to the attitudes of apathy, absence and attack is that we should become catholic, with a small *c* as well as a capital. We must become rooted in a deep catholic tradition and take to ourselves the catholic or universal principles of a mankind to become so human that it will be more than human. We must face with complete honesty and sincerity these contemporary attitudes and ask what they mean and how they are related to our traditions of faith. Let me speak from this viewpoint first with reference to the notion of absence and then to the attitude of attack.

The religious cry of the absence or silence of God has multiple roots. Human sinfulness and the evil powers of the universe undoubtedly are partly responsible for it. Human progress and scientific discoveries perhaps made this development inevitable. But what Christians must be especially attentive to is the fact that behind these other causes lies Christianity itself that has brought on such a crisis of faith. From the beginning Christianity was a destroyer of gods and a depopulator of the heavens. Men had had a variety of religious faiths to fall back upon. The gods were at least close at hand even if not always cooperative with man. But Christianity in its conception of God could brook no opposition. Men of the ancient world were correct in perceiving that their world was being desacralized, that their gods were being killed, and that god was no longer to be a piece of this world. Not entirely without cause was the reaction cited, for example, in the *Martyrdom of St. Polycarp*: "The whole mob astonished at the heroism of the God-loving and God-fearing race of Christians shouted: 'Away with the atheists'."

Christian faith thus introduced within mankind a unique conception of God, a God of faith, a God beyond all earthly dreams and desires. Never had the world possessed such an exalted notion of God as the one which Christian faith presented. The question one might pose is whether this notion was too exalted to live with. God was so high above the heavens that he was beyond being; he was so much "to be" that he himself no longer existed. This terminology is not that of the contemporary radical left but that of St. Thomas Aquinas. The God of Christian faith, according to Aquinas, is *supra-ens,* not one of the objects of this world but the presupposition of them all. God does not exist; he does not have existence because he is "subsistent to be," the source and origin of all acts of existing.

This was a most profound understanding of God and God's relation to the world. But this was also a dangerous business that Christian faith had initiated: the insistence that *no* earthly image is commensurate with God and the conviction that the world possesses its own autonomy unmixed with the fates of the gods. Thus it has been in our own day, in the Christian era, that the oracles have become silent and men have become painfully aware that there are no divine words fallen from the sky which men can cling to as their salvation. "Holy words," wrote Heidegger, "are lacking to us." In this perspective, empirical science has simply hastened the process which Christian faith had begun: the desacralizing of the universe. Science has continually killed the idols that a superficial apologetic has kept placing in its path until today we have grown weary of constructing new gods and tired of protecting the old ones. Now in the midst of our privately constructed world of precepts, doctrines and devotions we hear: silence. As was true of Israel long ago, we have gotten more than we bargained for, which proves only that man is not in a position to bargain with God.

Silence can be a terrible thing—but not necessarily. Silence is part of the rhythm of personal existence, the point at which words fail to convey the deepest meaning. It is in silence that relation grows in the pre-verbal and sub-conscious levels of the interlocutors. Silence is possible only for a being that can speak. Rocks and rivers and trees are not silent; their lack of speech conveys nothing. But if the world does experience, even if among a few, the absence and silence of God, this is a most heartening reaction, because the experience of absence is not

91

at all equivalent to nothingness. To experience God's absence is a Christian phenomenon unthinkable without the presuppositions of creation, faith and redemption. The question for Christians is whether they are a match for this agonizing silence, whether like Christ on the cross they can cry out of the darkness without despairing.

The response of Christians today, therefore, must not be an attempt to plug the gaps with petty defenses, working more and more feverishly to stave off the advancing world. Instead, the life of Christian faith demands that the world be accepted in its totality in order that we may go beyond it. Undoubtedly, there is a danger of ending with a purely secularistic humanism and this is a danger never lightly to be dismissed. But, paradoxically enough, the danger of turning faith into a self-enclosed secularism is greatest precisely when the humanizing process is opposed in the name of faith. Those who try to escape from historical evolution and the struggle to improve the human condition do not succeed in choosing the divine over the human but only in idolizing the elements of a past human culture.

This consideration has already involved me in the response to the attitude of attack. I have said that the most profound difficulty of Christian faith in the modern era has been the fact that it was based upon negations. By seeing God's function as the forgiver of sin, by exalting faith at the expense of reason, by over-emphasizing selected institutional elements, post-reformational Christianity could not find God by going beyond man, because it could not accept man. Its belief in God was interwoven with a partial negation of human existence. As a result, it was left to non-Christian forces to take a stand in favor of man. This was the most devastating attack ever launched upon Christianity because it arose not from the outside but from the very roots of Christianity itself. Freedom, dignity, equality, personality—all of these Christianity had helped give birth to. Now they had come back to haunt the parent. What was needed in response was not a faith that could hold back the surge of human freedom. What was needed was a Christian faith that could recover its own roots and let loose humanity. Christian faith does not add to the human nor subtract from the human. It is rather what supports and gives ultimate meaning to the whole of human history. God does not intrude as a competing force in his creation; he is the beginning, end and presupposition of all experience.

This view of God's relation to the world requires something of a revolution in thinking for all of us. We have consistently based our faith upon the gaps in the world and the negations in human existence. Though we have become more sophisticated in recent years our approach is still an insertion of God through the crevices rather than the opening of man beyond himself to the God of hope and love. We still poke around in man's psychic entrails, and when we have men shaking a bit then we overpower them with a God out of the sky. Perhaps this approach is still effective to some degree; I would question whether it is. At any rate, it is unchristian and it fails to understand the historical position we are in. It fails to reground Christian faith in Jesus Christ who did not come around distributing solutions to problems but who took humanity as it was and lived human life to the end. God cannot be *used* today; neither can man. All that is left today is the total acceptance of both, the one through the other.

The argument of the Christian with atheism, therefore, cannot be that the atheist is too humanistic, but that the atheist is neither humanist nor atheist enough. "The total recovery of man by man" was a Christian program before it was Marxist. It must be carried beyond the point where Marxism leaves it. For in Communism man is not totally recovered, he is sacrificed to the idol of history. This last idolatrous god must also be destroyed; the way must be cleared for the emergence of a new humanity. This can happen only when Christianity finds its Creator and Lord of history who invites man into a personal relationship of faith and love, the one who stands in no need of us though we stand in desperate need of him.

What I have said up to this point can, I think, be generally applied to the problems of the adolescent. I will simply highlight some of these things as particularly relevant to a person of that age and development. The basic problem of man is in becoming human. As the church has always taught, one can become human only by becoming more than human. The adolescent in particular has this difficulty: he is in search of humanity and trying to find his own identity as a man. He could use a helping hand rather than a lot of people telling him what to believe and what to do. He cannot believe in God, because he does not believe in anyone, least of all himself. Or, rather, if we take into account all the levels of belief, there is in the adolescent a tenacious grasp upon God and upon his own experience, but he is so confused in his head that he cannot be fully aware of his belief.

What adolescents need is to find someone they can trust, someone they can be sure is not making a business out of them, someone who trusts them enough to desire the full expansion of their human potentialities. If becoming a mature adult means leaving behind the world of childhood, so much the worse for childish idols. If it means young people must pass through a death to childish faith, then this also means that they need the help of a mature Christian who will not push them but who will wait patiently while they find God on the other side of disbelief. It was only by dying that Christ rose to a new life, and what he could have used when dying was a little human consolation and not slick arguments to prove that he was incorrect in his experience.

The problem of the maturation of faith for child and adolescent is interwoven with the over-all difficulty of growing up in present-day America. The intense emotional feelings of childhood and adolescence will pass away and this should be to our advantage. Certainly, religious teaching ought not to be played too closely into their feelings. Any kind of religious revivalism among adolescents is, I would suggest, a highly risky and doubtful business. I would support the contention that any deeply felt experience which helps to open them out to the reality of living with other men in a world to be perfected unto God is all to be praised. But there is a certain kind of salesmanship of religion that plays upon young people's feelings without bringing to bear human understanding and control. This approach to children and young adults is, I maintain, not only useless but unchristian and inhuman. I would be more than a little skeptical of attempts to bring on an ultimate and total commitment to Christian faith as early as possible in the lives of students. Life must be kept multi-dimensional; they have to learn how to think from different perspectives and to choose beyond the worlds of illusion that their intense private feelings construct. Into this turbulent eruption of human flesh and psyche Christian faith cannot be inserted as the answer to their problems nor as the primary motive for their actions. Christian faith can only be the ultimate option that lies beyond the immediate physical and psychological struggle; not the answer to their problems nor an escape from their problems, but the ever calm invitation to find themselves and the real world of God and people by trust and by the love that overcomes fear.

It should hardly be surprising that in our society the experience of the absence of God hits the adolescent particularly hard. He exists at the crossroads of a Christian culture shedding its adolescence and his own biological frame racked by the pull of adulthood. Adolescents can no longer believe in their god, the god of their system, the god of Fellini's Juliet "behind the trap door covered with dust over the stage of the convent school." They can hold on to that god for a long while but when the door is finally thrown open they find neither god nor a ravaging spider but instead emptiness or open fields. Their utter amazement, confusion and despair at this absence spring partly from two faults of ours: (1) the mythical picture that all children have of God has been reinforced in every detail by teachers who thought they were building up a religious life, (2) what is worse is that when this picture begins to disintegrate as it surely must in our modern world we do not rejoice with them and urge them forward, but we try to make them return to childhood when in fact they have nothing to go back to.

Caught, as they are then, in the crossfire of religion and personality, their response to faith must largely be one of either apathy or attack. The apathy often springs not from a lack of concern about these questions but from a concern which is being protected by a defense wall. The one thing about Christianity many young people are sure of is that Christian faith has nothing to offer, that it shot its bolt long ago in their lives, that it has been tried and found wanting. And the more desperately the religious salesmen try to answer all adolescent problems with Christian faith the more the young people are convinced that faith is hopelessly and ridiculously irrelevant. They are being given the hard sell these days, which is for them the final reason that they should not buy. Their problems are deeply human, intensely physical, confusedly psychological; no cute system of immediate relief is even to be considered. When religious faith does appear to have something to say it is not to be trusted, for it has too often lied, mistaking fairy tales for facts, and confusing loyalty to ideals with blindness to faults. Thus in order to resist the temptation to Christianity one remains apathetic, and all attempts to break the barrier verbally succeed only in strengthening it.

The student, on the other hand, who openly opposes Christian beliefs and refuses to fulfill the demands of the church is, I suspect, not so different from the apathetic. Here there may be a tragic misunderstanding of Christian faith which makes it appear incompatible with the development of human personality; or there may be a suspicion of what Christianity demands and a fear to face it alone. Though they are outwardly so different, I suggest that apathy and attack both grow out of the experience of absence or loneliness. I am further suggesting that the breakthrough must come from adult human beings and most preferably from a dedicated Christian community. What those growing up so desperately need is a human being who will take them from where they are, who will believe in them to such an extent that they also will come to believe, who hold on with an adult love that will never overwhelm but will never let go.

My remarks in this essay may have sounded harshly critical of the past; I did not mean them to be so. Great numbers of priests, parents and educators have succeeded in providing the help toward Christian maturity that I have just described. The deepest and best influences of faith worked by these teachers have often been in ways unsuspected by the teachers themselves, sometimes even against their own words. While we should appreciate all that has been done in the past, it must still be said that there is need today for the teacher who is cognizant both of theological developments in the church and present changes in society. We need men who are trying to face candidly the difficulties of belief and who can live with a deep conviction of faith together with uncertainty regarding many individual points of faith. These are the men who can hold out some real ideal for the struggling adolescent. Adolescence ought to be a time of conflict and struggle; it is not for adults to play it safe by trying to avoid all conflict. But it is incumbent upon the adult world to see that the struggle of youth is a fruitful one. This means that the young must be aided by the light of human intelligence that is freed from its shackles of fear through the testimony of Christian life and understanding.

7. Hope: Foundation of Religious Education

NEARLY all Catholics who have received religious instruction know that there are three theological virtues: faith, hope and charity. They have been told more than once that the Christian life consists in the living of these three virtues. The Christian's direct relation to God through the theological virtues distinguishes and characterizes the Christian life. Most Catholics would be confident in saying that they know something of the virtue of faith. They are well aware that there is a body of truths to which the Christian must adhere. Similarly, the virtue of charity is easily known and appreciated if not always successfully practiced. Everyone knows that charity has to do with willing what is right, with treating our neighbor as ourselves, and with performing what God demands of us.

The puzzle for most Catholics who have ever given a thought to the matter is the role of the virtue of hope. At first sight there seems to be no place for a third virtue. Hope hardly seems to have the same status as the two great virtues of faith and charity. The only thing that students seem to know about hope is that presumption and despair are opposed to it. Once that has been said there seems to be little more to say.

That the ordinary Catholic should have little to say about the virtue of hope is hardly surprising, since the topic has been a stranger to pulpits and classrooms. With some justification hope has been called the "forgotten virtue." It would appear that even the greatest of Catholic theologians could think of little to say about hope. In St. Augustine's treatise on the theological virtues, 113 chapters on faith are followed by three chapters on hope. In St. Thomas's weighty Summa of 604 questions, only two of those questions discuss hope.

Given these facts, the title of this essay may seem somewhat strange. Is it possible that the unknown virtue of hope constitutes the very foundation of religious education? By answering this question in the affirmative I am not claiming that religious education in the past has been without a foundation. I am asserting, however, that this foundation is for the first time becoming fully explicit. Despite the fact that hope remains an unknown entity to many of the faithful, a tremendous flowering of theological activity has been taking place concerned with the virtue of hope. One might dare to predict that theology in the future may remember the twentieth century as the century that gave birth to the theology of hope. The recent publication of Jürgen Moltmann's book[1] has summed up the movement taking place in both Catholic and Protestant circles. This movement would maintain that one cannot understand Christianity unless hope is placed at the center.

The theology in the church today carries profound practical implications. This is particularly true of the theology of hope. Pastoral needs in the church have pressured much of the theological thinking. It is not an aesthetic desire to round off the treatise on the virtues which has given impetus to the theology of hope. Christian life in the twentieth century has made its development imperative. It is with one part of that pastoral side, namely, the catechetical, that I am concerned. First, I would like to show some of the developments of the theology of hope and to indicate that faith and charity cannot be fully appreciated without an understanding of hope. Second, I wish to show the signficance of this theology of hope for religious education; I would claim, indeed, that its importance can hardly be exaggerated.

1. *Theology of Hope* (New York, 1967).

FAITH AND HOPE

It is often said that faith is the aim in catechetical work.[2] This need not be denied by the insistence on the central importance of hope. Faith and hope are complementary and inseparable; it is impossible fully to understand one except through and with the other. Some people who oppose recent developments in theology and catechetics contend that current writing simply confuses faith and hope. They would claim that theology in the past gave separate but adequate treatment to each of the virtues. There would then be nothing new in talk of commitment or encounter in faith; just a reshuffling of the treatises. It is true that faith and hope are being studied together, but this is not mere methodological change and much less is it confusion. The issue quite simply is man's relationship to God. The theology manual that fails to show the union of faith and hope does not do justice to man's nature or Christian revelation.

If we turn to the new testament we find that the synoptic gospels do not have a word for hope. This would seem to belie the claim that hope is of central concern in Christian revelation. This peculiarity, however, is due to the fact that the word we translate as faith contains the chief elements of hope. In other words, the two attitudes which we express by the words "belief" and "trust" are found in a single word in the synoptic gospels. Belief and trust are inseparably united in the minds of the evangelists. Belief without trust would be sterile; trust without belief would be absurd. St. Paul expresses the idea of hope through a word different from faith but he never entirely separates the two. In numerous places in his writings the words "faith" and "hope" are practically interchangeable. In the famous eleventh chapter of the Epistle to the Hebrews, when

2. See Gabriel Moran, "Faith as Aim in Religious Education," *Catholic Educational Review* LXI (February, 1963), pp. 113–121.

the author comes to define what faith is, the one way he finds to do it is through hope: "Faith is the substance of things to be hoped for, the evidence of things which appear not." (Heb. 11:1).

The difficulty which we face in trying to understand the new testament teaching on faith and hope does not arise only from a linguistic problem. The difference in terminology here between the bible and later theology manuals is not a quirk of language. The two of them mirror different ways of thinking and acting. After centuries of Western rationalism we find it all but impossible to conceive of faith other than as assent to propositions. Even the most recent writing on faith, while trying to say something different, inevitably correlates "revealed truths" with faith.

The only way really to break out of this theology of faith is to see revelation as a process in which there is revealed *someone* rather than truths. Faith then becomes not the correlative of revelation but an attitude *within* a revelational process. To maintain that it is "people we believe in" exposes one to the charge of confusing the issue or using unscientific language. It is interesting to note that this primary meaning for faith, that is, "believing in people," was expounded both by St. Augustine and by St. Thomas Aquinas.

The point I wish to stress here is that so long as faith is thought of as adherence to truths, then hope will never be understood. The only meaningful way to see faith and hope is as surrender of one person to another. The new testament writers saw no difficulty in relating faith and hope; the two could be distinguished but within the same unified reality. To believe in Jesus is to count on Jesus' goodness and look for salvation. The act by which a man takes up his position as a Christian is an act of trust that includes a yes to Christ's teaching. Believing in someone means accepting the truth of what he says and the promises that he makes. Although it is legitimate to distinguish these elements for purposes of study,

101

the interrelation of them must not be lost sight of or the whole Christian life will suffer.

THEOLOGY AND HOPE

Hope is, therefore, one of the main themes of Judaic-Christian revelation. Indeed, it is possible to distinguish the old testament from other religions by this single attitude of hope. Primitive religions, as Mircea Eliade has shown in his studies, are characterized by their withdrawal from history and their denial of the temporal process. Man in primitive society, living without hope in the future, was incapable of facing the "terrors of history" and was forced to live in a world of unchanging archetypes.

It was the Judaic-Christian tradition that taught men to hope. It initiated the belief that men are not alone but that as a part of the whole human family they move toward a goal in time. Only on the basis of this belief could history be viewed as progressive rather than cyclical. The old testament has rightly been called the primitive history of hope, the movement of God's people toward a promise. Christians believe that the promise to the Jewish nation reaches a fulfillment in the person of Jesus. The end was reached and the end was Christ. In his bodily self was the beginning of the regime of *shalom*.

The hope of the Christian is also a looking to the future. The difference lies in the belief that the decisive battle has been won. The risen Christ, the first great emigrant of the new testament, has become the embodiment of man's hope. Through his relation to Christ man has some access to the risen life even here on earth. Hope though directed to the future has effects that extend into the present. "It is in hope that we *are* saved" (Rom. 8:24). The straining forward of all creatures toward the final manifestation of glory is in confident expectation that the material universe is being redeemed. In the time of waiting

102

after the Ascension the church marches (or straggles) forward. Toward the end of his life Dietrich Bonhoeffer wrote: "The risen Christ bears the new humanity within Himself, the final glorious 'yes' which God addresses to the new man. It is true that mankind is still living the old life, but it is already beyond the old. It still lives in a world of death, but it is already beyond death. It still lives in a world of sin, but it is already beyond sin. The night is not yet over but already the dawn is breaking."[3]

Christian theology is a reflection upon revelation that had already begun in apostolic times. This word of reflection and interpretation gradually became more systematic. The development of a systematic theology, however, did not follow a logical pattern. It was dictated by the needs of the Christian community and particularly by the necessity of clarifying those doctrines jeopardized by heresy. As a result, some parts of theology were highly developed while other parts were only sketchily worked out. It may be said without exaggeration that no part of theology was more lacking in development than the virtue of hope. From what has been said so far it should be clear that the failure to appreciate hope is particularly bad in that it is symptomatic of great deficiencies in other parts of theology. It would be a fascinating study but one beyond the scope of this essay to trace the connection between a poor theology of hope and an inadequate theology of grace, revelation, christology and ecclesiology.

The two great themes which characterize hope throughout the biblical tradition are its communal nature and its historical dimension. Hope is almost never used in either the old or the new testaments except in reference to a community, a people, a church. In like manner, hope pertains essentially to an historical event, that is, to the action of God in time. What is unfortunate about scholastic theology is that it was precisely these two characteristics which were lost sight of. Theologians

3. *Ethics* (New York, 1965), p. 79.

seemed to have lacked instruments subtle enough for grasping hope in its rich and concrete fullness.

Early Christianity had looked forward to a speedy return of the Lord. They awaited with confidence the final event, the parousia. When it was realized that the parousia might not be so imminent as had first been assumed, the doctrine of the last day was no longer emphasized. It is true that the theme of growth of the City of God retained a certain primacy throughout the patristic period. However, the sense of the historical seems to have declined at least after the age of Augustine. With this change hope tended to become more vertical than horizontal, that is, more centered on the "salvation of my soul" than on the day of the Lord and the completion of the body of Christ. A de-emphasis of the social was inevitably joined with a loss of the historical. Thus, in an almost complete reversal of what the scriptures had to say, theologians denied that hope could be anything but hope for oneself. Despite the correctiveness that St. Thomas applied and the relation he established between hope and charity, his work could not overcome the deficiency. Late scholastic theology was not only lacking a theology of hope, it was unaware that it needed one.

The renaissance period was ripe for the reawakening of hope, but it was the human sciences which filled the void. The possibility of bettering the social conditions was made available in man's mastering of science and technology. The unchecked success of the physical sciences issued in a remarkable belief in the inevitability of progress. With Hegelian philosophy and the study of history, this consciousness of historical evolution was considerably sharpened in the nineteenth century. Finally, Marxism appeared as a logical counterposition to Christianity. The two great themes it proclaimed were historical process and communal sharing. The characteristics of biblical hope thus reappeared but the biblical God had been removed.

The twentieth century seems to represent a change in attitude about the inevitability of progress. Since the First World War there has been widespread disillusion with the sciences and widespread fear at the perilous situation of man. Camus may have exaggerated when he wrote: "Our generation's one demand is to get on equal terms with despair,"[4] but he was surely closer to the truth than the man of today who thinks that the world is improving a little each day and assumes that it must continue that way. If it is not the time for despair, it is at least the time for grave concern over whether man can control the forces he has created.

For the advent of Christian hope it is not necessary that men first despair; it is only necessary that men realize the ambivalence of all human hopes. This it would seem is being accomplished in the twentieth century. Man is being awakened to his lack of self-sufficiency and thereby to his true position of limitation and weakness in a universe not of his making. This ambivalent era thus offers a fertile ground for the growth of hope. "The truth is that there can strictly be no hope except when the temptation to despair exists. Hope is the act by which this temptation is actively or victoriously overcome."[5] The old gods have died and idols no longer satisfy. Man will soon have to choose between the Christian God and a purely secular hope. Belief in the former was never very easy but belief in the latter is also having its troubles these days.

The social questions of the modern world have forced the Christian theologians to examine the communal structure of Christian hope. The biblical and liturgical movements have produced a deeper understanding of hope than had ever been attained before. More specifically, it is from the study of the resurrection and a better understanding of the sacraments that the theology of hope is emerging. Man's hope is in the risen Christ who has entered behind the veil of heaven and who

4. Albert Camus as quoted in A. M. Carré, *Hope or Despair* (New York, 1955), p. 1.
5. Gabriel Marcel, "A Sketch of a Phenomenology and Metaphysics of Hope," in *Homo Viator* (Chicago, 1951), p. 36.

continues to exercise his priesthood in man's behalf. There is little use in telling Christians that they should hope. What hope presupposes is that Christians have met and have come to know Jesus their high priest. If Christian piety were centered there, then Christian hope would undoubtedly follow.

CATECHESIS AND HOPE

This developing theology of hope is of incalculable importance to the work of religious education. Insistence upon hope does not mean adding a certain number of class periods of instruction on the virtue of hope. What it does mean is that a catechist must come to understand hope and must see it as the support of his teaching.

Every human work is begun with some kind of hope, that is, with a desire to attain some objective and with a reasonable expectation that it can be reached. The work of religion teaching is undertaken each year by hundreds of young men and women enthusiastic over their work and eager to achieve great results. It is a sad thing to see how many of them become disillusioned with this work in a very short time. Some of them switch to another vocation, others give up their "idealism" and settle into what they call a realistic outlook.

The realization that human hopes will not be fulfilled in religion teaching is a step in the right direction. The mistake of those who despair of achieving their expected results is not in losing human hope but in failing to develop the virtue of hope that springs from Christian revelation. Hope is not a disposition or a vague feeling that "everything will turn out all right." The Christian virtue of hope is a life and life must be nurtured or else it will die. We do not necessarily have hope; it is a gift which can be received, can be developed, and can be lost. Hope is neither an easy optimism nor a gloomy pessimism; the former is just as opposed to hope as is the latter.

The teacher who is formed in hope puts himself at the service of the community fully aware that there may be little visible effect of or reward for his work.

To hope is to look on a child with the eyes of God. God is he who sees man in all the unrealized potentialities of his being. In this view every child is a world of infinite worth. No effort is useless or futile that may advance the child one step in the direction of God's designs. No one needs to be told how difficult it is to maintain such an outlook. Nevertheless, this is the role of the catechist: to view each child as the child of God.

The acceptance of a person in this way is the strongest factor making for change in that person. On the other hand, to say that "such and such a case is hopeless" is never justified. Man is not in a position to make such a judgment. In addition, the judgment itself can have very harmful effects. The worst thing about a teacher despairing of a student is that it may lead the student to despair of himself. To hope in another is to help the other to realize his best possibilities. To despair of another is to stifle this creative process and to deprive him of his possibility of invention.

Hope is revelatory of oneself. Man discovers himself not in meditation upon his own ego but in communion with others. Man by himself against the world is a helpless, almost absurd little creature. But if man recognizes his union with all men before the Absolute Person who brought mankind out of nothingness, then man can no longer consider despair in any terms except treason.

For men to realize this relation to God and neighbor, there must be a communication of Christian faith in its integrity. Although imposing external practices and threatening against sin may seem to be more "realistic," faith and hope will never be attained by that route. A propagandist tries to make exact copies of himself. He tries to make man in his own image and likeness. "Propaganda's essential character is a lack of expectant

107

hope and an absence of due humility."[6] A catechist, on the other hand, can only try to awaken in another the consciousness of his divine filiation. There are no infallible ways of doing this and our very best efforts may seem to fail completely. What is not to be forgotten here is that books and definitions are not of much help. The normal expression of trust is not found in a formula but in the action of a person.

The great significance of hope, therefore, is its social character. It is through hope that the faith and charity of our students will impregnate the world. The grossest error concerning hope is to think that this virtue is a kind of quietism that tolerates social evil in the name of an other-worldly recompense. If there is some truth to Marx's charge that "religion is the moan of the oppressed creature, the sentiment of a heartless world, as it is the spirit of spiritless conditions," this is not due to an excess of Christian hope but to a lack of it.

There are "spiritualities" which claim to be Christian and which seem quite unconcerned with the world. But no Christian who grasps the meaning of the new testament can be oblivious to the great social problems of the day. Such problems will be attacked by our students when they become alive to the meaning of Christian hope. It is a hope that sees all men united in the redeeming of earthly reality. "It is the most active saints who carry hope to its highest degree; this would be unconceivable if hope were simply an inactive state of soul. The mistake so often made here comes from a stoical representation of the will as a stiffening of the soul, whereas it is on the contrary relaxation and creation."[7]

The other dimension of hope that is so important in religion teaching is its historical character. To face up to the social tasks of our time is to enter the stream of history and live as an historical being. To live as an historical being would seem to be an easy task; yet we know today how great is the tempta-

6. J. C. Hoekendijk, *The Church Inside Out* (Philadelphia, 1966), p. 23.
7. Marcel, *The Philosophy of Existentialism* (New York, 1962), p. 32.

tion for man to escape from the temporal process and live out his life in the unchanging patterns of his own mind. Without Christian hope, history can be a terrifying thing. Man is driven forward biologically and psychologically. His being is a continual dying that tends toward the ultimate dissolution of his being. Christian revelation is to help man live time in its fullness, facing up to its frightening anxieties and at the same time not despairing. Hope brings the future into relation with the present, thus giving meaning to the sufferings and trials of men. The church's life of fidelity and trust is the organ and the veiled manifestation of the life that is to come.

Just as hope implies a confident expectation of what is to come, it also includes the acceptance of the fact that this end can be reached only by the rhythm which life itself dictates. Children must grow into a life of faith and hope; it cannot be simply created and it certainly cannot be imposed. This requires a great deal of patience both with ourselves and others. We are always tempted to deny the historical character of man and to skip intermediate stages. We wish to see results and we wish to see them now. A message of hope delivered in a patient manner does not produce many glamorous results. But at the root of all great and valuable work there is a calm hope and patient expectation. "There can be no wisdom which is not the fruit of a slowly developed maturity, and maturity presupposes patience and continuity. . . . He who would obtain everything from himself and this immediately will never attain to wisdom."[8]

CONCLUSION

Everything depends today on whether Christianity can communicate hope to a world that often feels hopeless before the forces it has created. Hope must move outward from family,

8. Marcel, *The Decline of Wisdom* (London, 1954), p. 40.

liturgy and classroom. No human reasoning will do it; hope can be communicated only in the life of faith.

For a religion teacher to carry out his task while respecting the autonomy of the student there is needed the virtue of hope. Immediate and easy fruits of success cannot be the goal of the catechist. With hope as the foundation and atmosphere of religious education, students will gradually acquire a mentality that sees creation with the eyes of God. It is the lives of these students that will bring other men to God most readily. What Christianity needs are men who grounded in faith and animated by charity are willing to live a life of hope.

8. Charity: Life of Religious Education

FROM the first moment of Christianity's existence there has never been any doubt that love of God and creation is the meaning, purpose and life of the Christian religion. This has been true despite the contrary impression often generated by the actual practice of Christian people. To the question of which is the greatest virtue, the new testament and the history of Christian thought give the same answer: charity. Even St. Paul, who places such emphasis on faith as the center of Christian life, leaves no doubt that charity as the living manifestation of faith is the fulfillment of the law and the high point of Christian existence.

The centrality of charity is crystal clear. Where Christians have often erred, and where they continue to err, is in assuming that it is self-evident what charity is. The difficulty in Christian living is often presented as a struggle of the higher against the lower in man. We seldom realize that a large part of our difficulty is that we do not know the good we are seeking. We constantly fail to take the proper road to charity because we are not seriously seeking to get insight into what charity is. "It is true that everybody everywhere talks about love. But the individuals who really know how to love are actually very rare. They are much rarer even than those who really know how to think."[1]

At the risk of merely saying more words about charity, I would like to offer some considerations about charity and how it is related to religious education. Charity is not the immediate and direct aim of religious education. This is not to denigrate

1. Ignace Lepp, *The Psychology of Loving* (Baltimore, 1963), p. 5.

the role of charity but to indicate that charity even more than faith is not something that is taught but something that is lived. To say that charity is not the immediate aim of teaching is far from saying that charity should not be the constant concern of teachers.

HUMAN FOUNDATION

One of the frequent failings of past theological and catechical writing was the neglect to study human foundations. We speak badly of God because we reflect superficially on our experience with men. If charity is the "form of all the virtues" and the greatest of God's gifts, then human experience must be structured in such a way that it is open to this completion. Divine love is not arbitrarily placed upon a nature which is foreign to it. All human love must in some way foreshadow and open out toward divine charity.

Man is that being whose reality is to be related to everything We assume that the more separated a thing is from everything else, the more truly it is itself. Actually, the reverse is true: "The more really special a thing is, the more abundance of being it has in itself, the more intimate unity and mutual participation there will be between it and what is other than itself."[2] Man's being is a "being toward" and a "being with." This is more than a fanciful way of saying that man has contacts with the world about him. It means that man is structured by his relations to the world and that these relations are constitutive of his being. Man is ontologically bound to the world; he reflexively discovers himself absorbed in the destiny of the world and driven by a thirst he cannot completely understand.

Man cannot escape his freedom even if he tries to do so and he often does. He is not free not to choose; his choice is

2. Rahner, *The Christian Commitment*, pp. 77–78.

either to affirm his relation to others and open himself to deeper communion or else to deny his true self and attempt self-sufficiency. "In the long run, all that is not done through love and for love must invariably end by being done against love. The human being who denies his nature as a created being ends by claiming for himself attributes which are a sort of caricature of those that belong to the uncreated."[3] Such an opening to communion with other men is not an easy task. It is fraught at every step of the way with fear of the loss of oneself. At every level of human relations there is a death which must be undergone before a new life can be reached. There is a courage needed to break out of the narrow circle of egoism and seek the good with others.

Man finds himself in the knowledge and love of other persons. Not only is community not the opposite of individuality, it is the indispensable, complementary pole. Only when a man comes to recognize the free autonomy of another does he attain the exercise of his own freedom. It must be recognized, however, that the other person always retains the element of threat to one's own freedom. Thus there is always the temptation to reduce the other to an object which can be manipulated. Human love is a precarious undertaking always exposed to bad faith. The analysis of love as sadism-masochism would have some persuasiveness if there were nothing higher than man and no greater love than man's.

A man discovers himself in addressing another; he speaks only to that which can answer him even if it be only by meaningful silence. The word which is spoken in love will find a response in another to help him overcome the barriers which cut him off from communion. To love is to accept the other in his autonomy and in all the uniqueness that makes him a person. This means that I cannot accept another unless I accept all the other relations which help to constitute his person. Thus, St. Thomas remarks that if you truly love your friend

3. Marcel, *Men Against Humanity* (London, 1952), pp. 55–56.

you will love his children. The test of authentic love is its centrifugal character. True love tends to spread outward and eventually to move toward communion with all.

Love preserves and saves the world. Far from being super-added to law and justice, love is responsible for all the justice in the world. It alone has power over the world because it seeks no power. The world needs a love that is truly human, but it is impossible to create love on a world-wide scale unless it is incarnated in individuals. What is needed today as always is the courage to work with individuals to awaken human love. "I cannot protest too strongly against the notion that our thinking nowadays is only valid if it is on a world-wide or planetary scale. Here, as elsewhere, it is the sense of the neighbor that needs awakening, for it is the only safeguard against calamities which indeed are certain to by world-wide."[4]

Scriptural Basis

What sharply distinguishes Judaic-Christian revelation from other religions is the utter mastery and control that God has over creation. There is at the beginning of things neither fall, nor struggle, nor accident; there is nothing but an act of sheer gratuity. God creates in order to give and to love; no cause can be assigned to the act by which he creates. From the first words of Genesis to the last scene of Revelation, the theme is God's love and what it produces. "God saw that all that he had made was very good" (Gen. 1:31).

God went further than the creation of a world. He willed that there should be free beings who could not only receive his love but return it to him. Even when man refuses to admit this dialogical relation to his creator, God does not cease to

4. Marcel, *The Decline of Wisdom*, p. 56.

call out to him. The old testament shows God choosing for himself a nation that would reveal his love to all people. The relation between Yahweh and Israel was never merely juridical; it was a continuing call of mercy and love to a faithless and faltering people. "I will pity 'Her-who-is-unpitied'; and I will say to 'Not-my-people,' 'You are my people'; and he shall say, 'My God'" (Hos. 2:32). By the shattering of earthly security and the recalling of divine promises, the prophets preached a religion of the heart. God, the faithful one, was preparing for a definitive affirmation of love. But the Israelite tended to fall back upon the security of the law; "ready to be a servant he was already a son without realizing it."[5]

In the person of Jesus Christ God made his irrevocable bond with the universe. Christ is the face God turns toward the world. God's love is poured out upon us; his will to save us is definitively affirmed in the resurrection-ascension. "A tree is known by its fruits, and men when they saw the divine *agape* of Christ shining in his works recognized that the kingdom of God was come."[6]

This divine *agape* revealed in Christ is benevolent, disinterested and efficacious. Man cannot produce such love but he can share in the love bestowed on Christ. The proof that man is sharing in that love which originates in God is the love that he has for his neighbor. Love of neighbor is not a second command in the sense of being added to the first. Rather, the love of man is the visible expression and surest sign of the love of God. The same dedication and service are the mark of love of God and love of man so that "if anyone says he loves God but does not love his brother, he is a liar" (1 Jn. 4:20). All that is not inspired by love is worthless; on the other hand, the whole law is fulfilled in one word: Thou shalt love they neighbor as thyself.

5. Rahner, *Theological Investigations* Vol. I (Baltimore, 1961), p. 122.
6. Ceslaus Spicq, *Agape in the New Testament* Vol. I (St. Louis, 1963), p. 132.

THEOLOGICAL REFLECTIONS

All love is from God whether it be the natural tendency of the appetitive power or the sharing of divine life by the indwelling Spirit. There can be in principle no conflict between authentic loves. Every true love is a movement toward God and likewise to love another for God's sake is to love what is most personal in him. Either man will love God, his neighbor and himself or else he will love no one. Man loves God by loving his neighbor and he cannot truly love his neighbor without loving God. Since one love implies the other a conflict of the two is based upon illusion or misunderstanding. "It is probably impossible to love any human being simply 'too much'. We may love him too much in proportion to our love of God, but it is the smallness of our love for God, not the greatness of our love for man that constitutes the inordinacy."[7]

C. S. Lewis remarks that we have often pressed upon Christians the duty of getting beyond earthly love when their real difficulty lay in getting so far.[8] This is usually put in the form of a condemnation of self-love. But genuine self-love is not only permissible, it is desperately needed. The preaching of self-hatred as the way to Christian holiness produces the worst narcissistic illusions while it accentuates dangerous neurotic tendencies deep in the human personality. Selfishness and self-love have often been equated whereas in fact they are opposites.

The way to love of God and love of neighbor, therefore, lies not in the quixotic attempt to negate the self. It comes from the awakening of the sense of the other and in the free turning to the absolute self. When a man begins to love all of God's creation (including himself) then self-love will take

7. C. S. Lewis, *The Four Loves* (New York, 1960), p. 170.
8. *Ibid.*, p. 165.

116

care of itself. Man knows himself in knowing another person; in like manner, he loves what is his true self only in loving another. If he does not love anyone else he will flee from his own freedom and end by destroying what is most personal in himself.

The foundation of Christian charity is the recognition of a man's position before God and his relation to every other man. Love that is natural to man is a mighty force that must be integrated into divine charity. Love promises more than it can deliver. Although one can rejoice in the genuine humanitarian impulse of our times, love can be demonic because it is infected with a selfishness which no one fully escapes. Because none of us sees the world as it really is and because none of us conquers his own failings, then anyone who proclaims himself the friend of all humanity must take care that he is not deceiving himself.

The motivation of love is inseparable from God's love for man, both in the fact of God's creating man and in God's adopting him as son. The reason why we are united in our humanity is that we have a common Father. Man is to love his brother because God loves him. No one is excluded since every man is the image of God. Even when it is not reciprocated, divine charity pours itself out without any eye to reward.

The charity which Christianity preaches complements the love that is part of the structure of human nature. A supernatural love without natural love is exposed to self-destruction because it is empty of concrete objects. No one is in worse danger than the "professional lover of God" who feels no emotion toward human beings and who disdains the value of human individuality for the sake of the "salvation of souls." What is desperately needed is a divine-human love, consumed with zeal for the kingdom of God yet patient with the failings of men; strict and unbending concerning the good of man yet respectful and tender in feeling; able to bestow out of a boundless sufficiency yet suffering and sympathetic with the

117

human condition. Such is the love that man has desired over the ages but cannot create on his own; such is precisely the love that Christianity claims has in fact been poured out upon the world.

CATECHETICAL CONSEQUENCES

The application of what is written above to the sphere of religious training is almost too obvious for saying. Yet the findings of modern psychology as well as the scriptural-theological doctrine of charity continue to run a poor second to the "practical" or "traditional" ways of educating children. One need not go so far as Mounier's description of education as the "massacre of the innocents" to protest that we are nowhere near achieving an education based on love rather than fear. Of course, everyone says that he is in favor of education by love. When it comes to practice, however, many teachers say that it is idealistic dreaming on the part of people who do not know children to say that they can be educated without fear and suppression. To this objection there is not a ready, convincing answer. All one can do is plead with educators to consider whether they really understand Christian charity, whether they are acquainted with well founded conclusions in child study, and whether they are certain that there are not untapped possibilities in the children they are working with.

The role of the teacher in the religious education of children should be in helping the child to discover and develop his own possibilities. In this way he can become a free and responsible person and not just any person but the one unique being envisioned by God. To foster that uniqueness of another and discover that place where freedom can become a creator is the greatest work a teacher can accomplish. "Genuine love is the most effective creator and promoter of human existence. If many persons who are well (or even moderately) endowed nevertheless remain mediocre, it is often because they have never been loved with a strong and tender love."[9]

The love of the teacher for his vocation and for his students is manifested throughout the whole process of educating. Whatever else teachers succeed in communicating to students, they do succeed in imparting the loves which dominate their own lives. Students never miss it even if they cannot explicitly state it. "You educate to some extent . . . by what you say, more by what you do, and still more by what you are; but most of all by the things you love."[10] Words spoken in love are what open human beings to other human beings, to other creatures and to God.

The autonomy of the human person must be respected at every level of development including infancy and childhood as well as adolescence and adulthood. There always have been and there will continue to be tensions between individual freedom and organizational structure. The church and its teachers will maintain this tension by the striving for free and responsible individuals. Although this principle may seem to be an empty truism to which everyone agrees (so that the only problem would be its practical implementation), the fact is that it is precisely the correct attitude toward freedom and responsibility that is often lacking.

It is not that we do not wish to love our students; far from it. We attempt to love them by protecting them from the dangers inherent in freedom. We feel so responsible for them that we take upon ourselves the molding of their moral lives. We prefer to form them upon a pattern of ideal human nature that has been given to us instead of allowing for the emergence of a unique personality that may not fit the laws of holiness we have conceived for ourselves.

The tragedy of this attitude is that it is self-defeating. One simply cannot choose for another nor save him from choices.

9. Lepp, *op. cit.*, p. 32.
10. F. H. Drinkwater, *Telling the Good News* (London, 1960), p. 169.

119

One can prepare external conditions, one can treat another with respect and love, one can try to awaken the consciousness of a call toward God and fellow creatures. But it would approach blasphemy to suppose that one can convert another, form his life, or make him love God.

The great enemy of love, according to the bible, is not hatred but fear. The whole church and especially the school ought to be concerned with diminishing fear. The school's contribution here is to give people "a feeling of what it is like to turn one's full intelligence on a problem, to think creatively, originally and constructively instead of defensively and evasively. We can hope that they will enjoy the experience enough to want to try it again; but it is only a hope. To put it another way, we can try to give them a glimpse of an intellectual foreign country, and even persuade them to visit it for a while; but it would take more time then we have to make them citizens of that country."[11] This sounds like a very modest aim but it is nonetheless a large order for any teacher. The key element will always be the experience of a strong human love that opens out richer possibilities while not doing away with direction and guidance.

The important thing is indeed charity but charity comes from God and the free response of human beings. Teachers could contribute some understanding and some of the conditions which will aid the flowering of human personality. On this point, what Carl Rogers says of his work would apply to the religion teacher: "In the most real moments of therapy I don't believe that this intention to help is any more than a substratum on my part either. Surely I wouldn't be doing this work if that wasn't part of my intention. And when I first see the client, that's what I hope I will be able to do, is to be able to help him. And yet in the interchange of the moment, I don't think my mind is filled with the thought of 'now I want to help you.' It is much more 'I want to understand you.'

11. John Holt, *How Children Fail* (New York, 1964), p. 27.

. . . Who are you? It seems to me that is a desire to meet a *person* not 'now I want to help.' It seems to me that I've learned through my experience that when we *can* meet, then help does occur, but that's a by-product."[12] If love means affirming a person in his own uniqueness, then help will come through meeting him because the meeting makes possible a self-affirmation. If we really are filled with trust and love we will be content in our roles as modest precursors of the one Catechist.

12. See the Appendix in Martin Buber, *The Knowledge of Man* (New York, 1965), p. 176.

9. Teaching Catholic Morality

I WOULD like to make some remarks on three aspects of this very complex subject: (1) the doctrinal foundations of Catholic morality, (2) the role of freedom in teaching for moral maturity, (3) the personal and social dimensions of Catholic morality.

Concerning doctrinal foundations, it should be fairly obvious that the question of teaching morality is tied up with the whole of Catholic theology, that is, with our understanding of the relation of God and man. One of the reasons we have poor catechetical presentations of morality is that we lack a fully developed moral theology. Or, I would prefer to say that we lack a theology with moral consequences. Moral theology has had a rocky history from the start. One often reads romantic stories about the breakdown of moral theology in modern times and the need to restore the great syntheses of the past. As a matter of fact, however, such a moral theology has never existed. Moral considerations grew up outside of theology and they have never been successfully integrated. The main lines of a moral theology were laid down by St. Thomas but his suggestions made slight impact on the actual development and teaching of morality. Only today is a Christian presentation of morality in the making. It is in the process of being developed upon scriptural, liturgical, philosophical and theological foundations. The net result will be not the perfection of moral theology but its destruction. That is, the more that morality becomes theological the more Christian the theology will be and the less need there will be for a distinct entity called moral theology. As Charles Curran has said, the moral theologian today is intent on eliminating his occupation. The problem of how to teach morality can only be posed within the context of this theological questioning. This kind of questioning will not improve our teaching overnight but it is the only hope for a long-term resolution of our difficulties. It is easy to say what moral teaching should be: Everyone says today that we must teach positively instead of negatively; everyone says that we must teach a morality of response to God's call; everyone says that we must center moral teaching on charity and the imitation of Christ. Speakers at catechetical workshops always say these things and we always shake our heads in agreement. Although we resolve to be positive, to be Christocentric, to be charity-oriented, it still ends up the same old thing in the classroom. What we fail to see is the depth of this problem. What we are not ready to admit is the superficiality of our understanding of both God and man. The external coordination of the commandments around charity, the introduction of contemporary applications, and the use of gospel parables are not sufficient to improve moral teaching. It is not the convincing of students of the relation of Christian mysteries and moral action that is first needed but our own seeing of that stupendous reality.

The risk of theology and religion teaching always lies in discussing things which no longer need discussion, speaking in a language which no one really understands, and failing to consider the questions and problems which real people have. What happens too often is that we do not speak to the people we are addressing. We speak the language of another century. When we meet with no response on the part of our hearer we are tempted to conclude that it is all due to bad will on his part. We deal very much in meaningless words, but though everyone is opposed to a meaningless vocabulary, few are willing to admit that this is a symptom and not the disease.

We are quite aware that the teaching problem is not solved by adding moral precepts to a dry, inspirationless doctrine. But

123

getting rid of the precepts or replacing them with something flashier does not get down to the roots of the problem. It is that half-digested study of doctrine that must come alive through more and better reflexion. We all want to teach our religion in simple, meaningful, and concrete terms; but we are mistaken if we think that it is a simple thing to teach our faith simply. It requires deep study and patient honesty on our part to show simply and without artificiality how the moral life of a Christian springs from belief in God revealed in Christ. The kind of development needed requires time, effort and cooperation; though there are many short cuts they will all eventually fail.

It is sometimes said that modern catechetics is downgrading the teaching of morality. It is in fact true that few articles in catechetical journals treat moral teaching explicity. On the other hand, I think it could be maintained that almost the whole of modern catechetics is concerned with nothing but morality. The difference today is the insistence that it be Christian morality, Christian in origin and end. Morality needs a religious life out of which it can grow organically. If we do not succeed in awakening within people what it means to be a Christian, then despite resolutions to the contrary, moral teachings will degenerate into lists of do's and don't's. Laws without a faith context and moral rituals apart from understanding are the most cunning enemies of freedom. "Even the law of the gospel would kill," writes St. Thomas, "if it be separated from the animation of the Holy Spirit."[1]

The solution to all our problems is God; "but," writes Rahner, "God must be God and not another name for the splendour of our own self disposing."[2] God must be he who stands in no need of us though we stand in desperate need of him. If we are not struggling forward to discover this God in his revelation, then morality will fall back upon itself and simply become patterned on human society. We blaspheme by

1. *Summa Theologica*, I–II, q. 106, a.2, c.
2. *Theological Investigations*, Vol. II, p. 93.

placing God in a sociological matrix with a set of rules agreed upon by both sides. Wo do not need God to make rules; the only thing we need God for is for there to be anything at all. It is not that students do not know the rules of the game, it is that they know neither God nor man sufficiently well.

The fruitless arguments of the past over whether religion teaching was to instruct students in doctrine or to form their moral lives could not have arisen if we had better understood God's revelation. We would never have formulated the question in those terms. Our task is neither doctrinal instruction nor moral formation; both of them are less than Christian, less than human. The task instead is to try to convey what it means to be a human person in the light of Jesus of Nazareth. "Given this knowledge," Jungmann writes, "one need not worry whether there will be a religious life to match it, simply because this kind of knowledge and appreciation of religious truth can only develop when there is an accompanying cultivation of religious life."[3]

This leads to the second major concern of this essay, the development of freedom for moral maturity. Whenever cate-chetical theorists sit around and talk about morality the point they stress is the necessity of freedom. On the other hand, when teachers hear such talk they wonder what this freedom is supposed to mean in a class of forty-five or a school of fifteen hundred.

Several points should be made in clarification. First, no one is proposing lawlessness or lack of order as an ideal. All people, but children especially, need rules and laws. No one who understands St. Paul would appeal to him for a contrary doctrine. Furthermore, it cannot be proposed that an individual teacher initiate theories of his own if they are entirely out of line with the rest of the school. For better or worse we are part of an organized community and what we do is determined

3. Josef Jungmann, *The Good News Yesterday and Today* (New York, 1962), p. 113.

within given limits. What is being asked for, however, is a careful and continuing examination of conscience on the part of both school and teachers as to whether they are intent on fostering the individuality of the student and whether they have clearly before their minds the fact that laws are for the sake of aiding freedom. The decisive question is not how many or how few the laws but whether the laws have a faith context and whether these laws help toward freedom and maturity. The Catholic school and the parish have often been lacking in wisdom on this score. Canon Drinkwater, with many years of experience behind him, remarks: "The older generation of priests and teachers, so much better in many ways than we are, made one enormous mistake—they often relied too much on compulsion instead of fostering the real tiny inward spark of faith. They felt so responsible for the children, and they expressed that feeling in the only way they knew."[4]

Students are not going to start acting freely when they leave high school or college. Freedom has to be cultivated from their earliest years. It is so much easier to impose ourselves upon children and get them to produce the kind of action that we consider morally good. We tend to think that any way in which the child differs from the adult is an evil that must be speedily corrected. In adopting such an attitude, which cancels the child's personality, the adult is convinced of his own love, zeal and sacrifice. Adults do not see the harm they are unconsciously doing. "If a child carries out the will of a teacher because he is afraid or because his affection is exploited, he has no will and obedience that is secured by the suppression of the will is truly oppression."[5]

I have heard teachers bemoan the fact that though it is easy to get students in early years of school to perform all kinds of religious practices, they suddenly change and often refuse to carry out minimum obligations. In Fichter's study of the

4. *Telling the Good News*, p. 153.
5. Maria Montessori, *Education for a New World* (Madras, 1959), p. 85.

126

Catholic school he found a great enthusiasm for religion in the second grade but almost none in the sixth and seventh grades.[6] Our problem is not they grow up, but part of our problem is that their religion has not helped them to grow up. Too much was impressed upon them too soon. Little children should not be loaded down with or subtly encouraged to adopt religious practices which raise up a façade around them.

There is another danger which seems poles apart from the preceding but it could involve the same error on our part. It is well known that adolescence is a period of paradoxes and contrasts, most strikingly so in the area of authority. The adolescent wants freedom but really not too much of it. He rebels against his elders but desperately needs their help and guidance. He detests all law, yet is the greatest lover of law. If he has no rules to follow he will create his own rituals and he can be severe in his judgments upon himself. In all of this he is highly idealistic in his moral striving.

We must make use of these tendencies; they are the raw material for holiness. But we must not trust adolescent moralism and we must not mistake it for holiness. Their perfectionistic striving is largely self-centered and their greatest moral danger is not sexual, as they usually think, but a phariseeism which must be overcome. We must not make the same mistake they do in thinking that Christian morality consists in overcoming nature by an anxious, soul-searching self-sufficiency. The task of the educator at this point is the creation of an atmosphere of devotion, self-forgetfulness and interest in others.

Part of the problem of a developing freedom is the crisis of faith, which I have dealt with in an earlier essay. I would only add here that it should not be assumed that such crises originate from moral failings. Statements have often been made that students who have intellectual problems of faith have been leading sinful lives and are only looking for an excuse to give up their faith. In some cases this is very likely true; as a

6. Joseph Fichter, *The Parochial School* (Notre Dame, 1958), chap. 4.

general rule it cannot be substantiated. The problem of many young Catholics today is that they would like to believe, but their religious life seems unauthentic and insincere.

Not all teen-agers have the grave problems which textbooks include in the chapter on adolescence. But enough of them do have this problem to make us realize that this is not a simple moral problem. It cannot be solved by intense argument or by shocked horror that anyone would dare call his faith in question. The young person must have the freedom to question in order to become an adult. This does not mean that parent or teacher must stand by idly and do nothing; but what is done must be done with an eye to mature freedom. The concrete steps that can be taken in an individual case will depend on all the circumstances.

It is useless today to gloss over the moral failings of Christians past and present or to meet every objection to faith and morality with a counter objection. Most of us recognize that this kind of apologetic was never very successful, but the young persons of today find this kind of thing repulsive. They will accept a sinful, suffering church abiding in God's merciful love. What they find difficult to accept is insincerity and a lack of forthrightness in facing up to unpleasant facts.

What we can do during this difficult period is often only small and indirect. It is a strain upon the faith of the catechist to work with patience and understanding and to be silent, to pray and to wait. Sometimes he appears to have great success; other times he must like Christ watch the rich young man turn away; at all times he must recognize that the lasting fruits of his work are invisible. He can do little to hasten the process. It must be a calm, continuing conversion in which the student grows out of his self-centeredness. To do this the student needs the example of persons who manifest in their lives a morality that is the definitive triumph of life over death, of beauty over ugliness, of love over all narrowness.

My third concern is the personal and social dimensions of

Christian morality. The Christian is always in a state of tension being in the world yet not of the world. It is always a battle on two fronts for the church: to avoid conforming to the standards which the world sets up but at the same time not to retreat from the mission to speak to the world from within the world. We are always in danger of fighting the wrong battles at the wrong time. We may spend most of our time today defending the rationality of Christianity and its compatibility with science when in fact this is not the main charge against Christian morality. From the time of Marx the attack upon Christianity has not been in the name of reason but in the name of humanity; the charge is not that Christianity is untrue but that Christianity is inhuman, depersonalizing and profoundly lacking in charity. This is an extraordinary indictment in that Christianity was to be the message of joy, freedom and personalization. We are tempted to dismiss the attack and say that they have misunderstood Christianity. Undoubtedly, they have but so must have a lot of Christians. "These Christians are a sad lot," said Nietzsche; "if they want me to believe in their savior, they will just have to sing better hymns."

Central to almost every movement of modern times is the human person. It was out of Christianity that the full notion of person emerged; it is on this basis that Judaic-Christian morality is capable of establishing a community of unique individuals. The teaching of personal morality requires that one start from people and that one end with people and that there be living people as examples. That may sound easy to do but for many of us it requires a revolution in attitude which cannot be accomplished simply by resolving to teach morality that way. To teach a morality that is personal, one must know the persons of the bible: the prophets, Jesus and Paul. In addition, one must know something of the key personalistic movements of our own day.

We must ask ourselves why so-called situation ethics is one of the dominant moral movements of our time. Is it because

129

people are just no good today, or is there some underlying moral aspiration here that we are not sufficiently aware of? An acquaintance with this movement might lead us to examine whether what we are teaching belongs to Christianity or whether some of it is simply a remnant of another age. Christian teaching cannot be absolved from all responsibility for the irrational explosions that characterize our day. A religion teaching that deals with human emotion only under the heading of "obstacles to free choice" must some day face the consequences of its denial of the human person.

If personal morality has always been tied to the social order it is only in our own day that this fact has become inescapably obvious. Any teaching on Christian morality must admit to the complexity of the social order and the rapidity of social change. Techniques for understanding, changing and using nature have been marvelously developed while the human structures have in many ways remained primitive. The social problems have become staggeringly complex. In this situation we have to remember Reinhold Niebuhr's warning to avoid the sin of trivia, that is, saying things which may be morally and doctrinally correct but which simply are not to the point. We have to avoid thinking that all we need do is repeat the simple, unchangeable answers we learned years ago, as if the acceptance of these answers would solve the world's social problems. We ought to stop talking about a Christian social doctrine in the sense of implying that we have some plan made out which the world refuses to accept; there is no such plan. What we ought to do is strive to understand the vast social movements and determine whether there is a relevant word we can say from the standpoint of our faith.

The church has no monopoly on truth; she does know of a truth which if operative in the world would make it a better place. But there is a difference between principles of justice and charity and the implementation of those principles. There is an oft-quoted story about St. Thomas that when someone asked him how to become a saint, he answered: Will it. In one sense this is true but taken at face value it is extremely dangerous. It must not be taken as a program of life nor be preached as the Christian answer to all questions. It is too easy to say that it does not matter what we are doing so long as it is for the love of God. It may not be enough today not to will evil and merely to sympathize with the good.

We must be careful about saying that the only thing lacking is charity. It is a serious and genuine question to ask: How do I practice charity? The answer of Christ in the parable of the good samaritan surely provides a profound insight. Nevertheless, every Christian must still ask: How do I go and do likewise in a highly complex society? Perhaps, as Teilhard said, charity will require us not only to bind up wounds but to be in the first ranks of the movement to change society. Much of our difficulty is not a lack of charity but a lack of facts: sociological, economic, political, psychological facts. For example, many people of good will fail to see the point in the struggle for civil rights for the quite evident reason that they have no facts to work with. This is more or less true of all of us and all of our students. If we had more charity we would be better men, but if we had a knowledge of key social issues we could express and develop the charity we do have. A lot of nice, sincere individuals do not necessarily make a good community. Unless the social structures are carefully understood and constantly changed, individuals will suffer; and it will all be in the name of sincerity and good will.

Everyone berates the moral theologians today for not solving our moral questions. Moral theologians are the first to admit their inadequacies but what are they to do? To write an adequate treatise on morality today would require one to be not only exegete, liturgist and theologian but also psychologist, economist and political analyst. Moral theologians lack facts, just as the rest of us do. I doubt that we can expect the rise of some individual who is going to be an expert in all these

131

fields. What then is to happen to the rest of us who are probably experts in none of these fields and yet must try to teach morality?

From what I have just said, there seem to me to be several inescapable conclusions. First, the teacher of morality to be an effective teacher must be interested in many other things besides moral. An obsessive concentration upon knowledge of moral precepts has never succeeded in reaching the real moral area. John Dewey's statement points up the problem: "If one could control the songs of a nation, one need not care who made the laws."[7] However short his time and limited his resources, a teacher has to try to acquaint himself with the society that his students live in, perhaps more with its songs than its laws. It is useless to educate students to live in a society that no longer exists. The assumption of moral responsibility takes place within the rather narrow limits that a society sets.

Second, anyone teaching morality must be ready when the occasion arises to do what he can to improve the social conditions. By vocation, teachers are talkers rather than doers, although a carefully chosen word can be an important form of doing. Andrew Greeley remarked some years ago that if liturgists want to improve liturgical participation, some of them should consider getting on city-planning councils. People having homes in which they can live like human beings would help not only liturgical participation but the state of social morality.

Third, teachers of morality must see that improvements in teaching morality demand an improved educational context. The student must come to religion study with some knowledge of history, economics or biology. The better the general education is, the greater is the possibility that morality will be well taught. The students we are educating cannot be social primitives incapable of working through established channels for relating Christian faith to the world.

7. *Freedom and Culture* (New York, 1963), p. 10.

Fourth, and perhaps most important, no matter how hard we try and how much things improve we cannot supply the answers to all the moral questions they will meet. Nor should we try. The school should strive to produce students who can grow with their faith. The components of moral maturity will be principles derived from concrete experience together with an adherence freely taken up in answer to Christ's invitation. The great moral questions are never going to be answered in the classroom, the pulpit or the confessional. They will be answered by educated laymen who can find answers in concrete situations and who are not afraid to trust their own judgments.

My conclusion draws together the three areas I have treated. There is an objection raised to teaching morality in the positive fashion advocated here. Are we not in danger of blurring the distinction between commandment and counsel; and thereby of adding obligations which God himself has not ordained? Must we not make clear what sin is and what it is not? When the objection is raised in those terms one is forced to admit that such a danger does exist, but the greater danger lies in people who are able to conceive morality only in those terms. What is wrong here is the underlying assumption of the objection, namely, that morality is co-extensive with commandment. When a person with this outlook is told to teach morality positively, the first thing he will do is restate the ten commandments positively. At best this is a rather trivial correction of God's teaching. He now has ten positive obligations but of course these are not clear-cut, and the great problem becomes how far one is obliged to honor property or to worship God. What is needed is not a rewording of the commandments but a reversal of moral attitude; not a positive attitude toward commandment but a positive attitude toward life.

We must get rid of the conviction that morality springs from obligation rather than vice versa. We must get rid of the assumption that the commandments from the traditional or only basis for teaching Christian morality. We must especially avoid

133

giving the impression that when one comes right down to it, the important thing is to keep those commandments; the rest of moral teaching being pious additions for those who have charity as well as justice. The use of the commandments may clarify what a sinful action is, and to know this is important. But the reason for saying anything about morality is to say how men might better live. Saying it in words will not be sufficient. When they see what a Christian life is and when they have come to hold it freely, then they will stop equating morality with obligations.

It is not that we have recently failed to educate Christians with such a moral outlook. Rather, it would appear that the church is only now reaching the stage where institutions are at hand to educate Christians in vast numbers. Perhaps the church is still in her infancy. God is patient with our stumbling efforts though often we are not. Wisdom, says Guardini, is a knowledge of the time that belongs to things; wisdom and patience are the same thing and man fully possesses neither of them. The era of Catholic moral maturity is before us if the teachers have sufficient faith and hope to sustain our movement forward.

10. From Children to Adults

ANYONE trying to theorize about religious education in America should be grateful for the Greeley-Rossi study, *The Education of Catholic Americans*.[1] The authors of this study of the Catholic schools modestly point out that the first consideration is not whether their scientific data are of high quality but whether there are any other data (p. 20). The policy maker in Catholic education, therefore, whatever his reservations about some of the conclusions and projections in this study, can still be appreciative of the many interesting statistics gathered together in this one volume.

There are, of course, severe limitations to a study such as this one. Most of the limitations are readily acknowledged by the authors themselves, although as they proceed to broad generalizations the limitations of their instruments sometimes seem to recede into the background. There is in the first place the obvious difficulty of measuring sociologically what constitutes a "better Catholic." The six measures that are designed to test the school's success in inculcating what it considered important Christian values afford only a partial insight into whether "better Catholics" were produced by the schools. It should be noted here, however, that this study has been unfairly criticized for equating better Catholics with those who maintain certain devotional practices. The authors are careful to insist that they are only trying to measure whether the school succeeded in doing what it was trying to do. Granted this stipulation, one might nevertheless question whether these meas-

1. Andrew M. Greeley and P. H. Rossi, *The Education of Catholic Americans* (Chicago, 1966).

135

ures are an adequate reflection of what the schools were attempting to do. For example, the measure of charity, which the authors say is religiously "the most important question that could be asked about Catholic schools," seems strangely truncated in its definition (pp. 66f.).

As one casts his eye over the points of doctrinal and ethical orthodoxy supposedly inculcated in religion classes, one might suspect that the failure of the school was at times traceable to the success of common sense and the Holy Spirit. The remark is not made cynically or facetiously. It is to point up the fact that the dedicated teachers in Catholic schools have often been much better than what they were saying in religion class. These teachers conveyed a sense of Christian living (sometimes in spite of what they were saying) but their success might be obscured or even be judged a failure on this sociological test.

In addition to the inherent difficulty of the subject and the fact that it is a measurement of the past rather than the present, there are limitations on the amount of data that can be collected for a single study. The authors admit that they lack information in some areas that would be needed to make more definite conclusions. For example, there is insufficient data to judge whether much of the Catholic school's effect is not simply the result of the selection and retention policies of the schools (p. 146). The recent Notre Dame study will therefore be helpful as a complement to this work for providing further factual information.[2]

It is now widely known that *The Education of Catholic Americans* does not provide a single clear answer concerning the success or failure of the Catholic school (p. 55). Widely divergent conclusions as to the future of the schools have been inferred from the data. This result has been a disappointment to some people who may have been unrealistically hopeful that such a study could produce startling data that would admit of only one interpretation. It seems to me, however, that the value

2. *Catholic Schools in Action*, ed. Reginald A. Neuwien (Notre Dame, 1966).

of the study lies in the very ambiguity of its conclusion, namely, that the schools are neither as good as some claim nor as bad as others claim. Although both sides of this two pronged conclusion may seem bland, the conclusion enables us to hold simultaneously to two positions which might appear opposed to one another.

The study, on the one hand, concludes that the Catholic schools are not so bad as some critics may paint them. The authors are confident that they can put to rest some of the charges casually tossed in the direction of the Catholic school today. They found no evidence that the schools are divisive (p. 154) or that they did harm to the educational and occupational achievements of their graduates (p. 140). If anything, the Catholic school graduate seemed to fare a little better in these areas than the public school graduate.

In the most delicate area of religious education the authors found that the schools did what was demanded of them and did it fairly well (p. 74). The schools, it is said, are unfairly criticized for failure to develop awareness of ecumenism or racial justice. The Catholic school was here only functioning as the faithful instrument of a church not especially attuned to these and similar issues. In religious training, therefore, the schools did what was asked of them with moderate success; whether something else should have been asked of them is a different matter.

This point would seem to be of value for those involved in the system of Catholic education. Many of those people have recently felt that they were in a state of siege, having been made the scapegoat for most of the ills of religious education. A situation of defensiveness and discouragement it not likely to be of help to anyone. The encouragement of being assured that they are doing something worthwhile might not be a bad thing for those in Catholic schools today. It could help to establish a better atmosphere for suggesting changes. In this context the criticism of the Catholic schools need not be taken as a belittling of their past accomplishments nor a destructive force relative to their present existence.

The other side of the ambiguous conclusion is that the schools are not so good as some proponents would claim. In the catechetical area the schools have not been the potent force they were often assumed to be. This fact helps us to recognize the need for further experimentation and perhaps radical changes in the educational pattern.

According to this study, the schools "have worked very well for those who would already be part of the religious elite; they have not worked so well for those whose religious backgrounds were less intense, and apparently, Catholics who have not attended them have not been appreciably harmed by their non-attendance" (p. 113). If this conclusion is correct, then we can proceed without fear to carry out experiments which might, for example, lessen the number of students in Catholic schools. The total impression this study conveys is that the way religious education is now carried out is terribly inefficient. Possibly this is the best we can do. It would seem, however, that serious changes might at least be tried to see if there are better ways.

The strangest thing about the Greeley-Rossi report is the authors' peculiar lack of imagination which leads them to conclude that despite the inefficiencies we must continue to pour all of the manpower, money and energies into what we have been doing in the past because there are no other proven alternatives. The question to be raised in this essay is not that of an alternative to the Catholic schools; rather it is that of beginning to channel some of our resources into other areas so that a new over-all approach to religious education can gradually emerge.

In our attempt to think through such a new pattern of religious education several of the findings in this study should be considered together. First, the connection between the religious atmosphere of the home and the effectiveness of the catechetical instruction is even closer than has generally been assumed. "For

138

all practical purposes, the religious impact of Catholic education is limited to those who come from highly religious families" (p. 85). Although the school may have a short-term effect upon all, any lasting effect is discernible only when the school is reinforced by family ties (p. 103). This does not mean that the schools simply duplicate the home; evidence is found that the school and home working in tandem accomplish more than either could alone (pp. 85ff.). That the school can only build on the attitude created in the home is not very surprising, but the percentage of homes that supplied this help is distressingly small. "If our data from the past are any indication of the present situation, Catholic education is virtually wasted on three-fourths of those in Catholic schools because of the absence of a sufficiently religious family milieu" (p. 112).

A second point of interest and importance is the need found for a comprehensive system of Catholic education. Significant effects seem to emerge only at the college level, but the college needs the preparation of Catholic education in primary and secondary schools. It is the cumulative effect of the sixteen years that is most important and not any one part of the system. The authors are therefore opposed to a concentration of effort on one level together with the elimination of part of the system. "A denomination considering a religious school system must face the fact that, if it really wishes such a system to be effective, it will be forced to ponder the possibility of its having to be comprehensive—from first grade to college" (p. 178). The study has some good things to say about the Catholic college and the effect of theology teaching even in the days prior to the modernization of theology curricula (pp. 169f.). At the college level the home is no longer so dominant an influence (p. 173). At this point there is some hope for meeting the student with a serious intellectual challenge that will lead to an adult faith.

A third area of findings that is perhaps the most disheartening is the failure of the schools to create a deep sense of social awareness, tolerance and community involvement. It has already been pointed out that the schools' effect here was not negative (as is sometimes implied) and furthermore that the lack of a significant positive contribution is more a failure of the church as a whole rather than the school. There is some inconclusive evidence that this situation is changing. This was indicated by the scores of the 20-year-old respondents on topics such as race and anti-semitism (p. 135).

The authors feel that if the schools were moderately successful in inculcating certain forms of behavior as being of "central symbolic importance" it should be possible to substitute other values today (p. 124). Perhaps this is true but the jump from one to the other may be greater than the authors assume. The issue here is not the replacing of one set of Christian things with another. A dominant theme of Christian theology today is the recognition that Christian faith is not a set of specific practices but a quality and direction of every human activity. Instead of simply substituting objects or "expanding values" the change may require an almost complete reversal of attitudes. The school's job in such a changed situation need not become unimportant but the function of the school becomes more limited, being mainly concerned with what a school can do well. This of course implies that the other agencies and institutions are going to be all the more necessary to provide things that had been perhaps unreasonably demanded of the school.

With these findings in the background I would like to draw several conclusions and make a few concrete proposals. It would appear that the two periods most crucial to religious development are the early life of the child and the searching years of young adulthood. Since the former is closely tied in with the development of the young adults who are or will soon be parents, these two tend to merge into a single question. In other words, the main catechetical question today concerns the adult world. This seems almost too obvious to say and yet the church's catechetical ventures seem more entrenched than ever in the world of the child, that is, in primary and secondary schools. It is true, as the authors of this study maintain, that the college will be effective only if the ground is prepared. I am not advocating that the church close down her primary and secondary schools. But surely there are priorities and there can be a shifting of emphasis within the total educational endeavor.

It might be a good thing if the church could provide sixteen years of excellent schooling for a large percentage of Catholic students. The fact is, however, that the percentage of students now receiving sixteen years of Catholic schooling is very small and no one seems to be predicting that it will not get smaller. Certainly the percentage is decreasing rapidly on the college level. We could conclude that this is most unfortunate and that we must use our energies to fight this decline.

The fact that the numbers are small is not conclusive proof that our efforts are misdirected. What is more distressing is the apparent inefficiency of a system that produces its effects in only one-fourth of that diminishing minority. Undoubtedly, much good is being accomplished and perhaps it is worth the energies and money being spent. But since there is only a limited amount of money and manpower available, one must ask whether a different set of priorities ought not to be established in a situation in which we simply cannot do all that we would like to see done.

The thesis several times enunciated in the book under review is that there is no proven alternative to the Catholic school system. This is obviously true but not entirely to the point. Catholics are advised in this study not to contemplate abandoning their educational system until by careful experimentation they can discover an equally effective alternative. This, the authors believe (as they reveal in the last two pages), will be never. And this might well be the case inasmuch as no widespread and careful experimentation is ever going to happen if nearly all the resources remain locked up where they are now. Furthermore, it is stacking the deck to ask whether there is an

141

alternative to the Catholic school system. The question is not an alternative to the school system but a different approach to religious education within which the Catholic school might take on a different role.

The Education of Catholic Americans deals only in passing with the work of CCD. The authors acknowledge that they did not gather much data in this area because they limited their study to the effect of Catholic schools. This is their prerogative. Their limited data, nevertheless, do not prevent them from making the following statement: "The romance of certain liberal Catholic writers with CCD is probably more the result of their own ideological (and personal) objections to Catholic schools than any solid proof of accomplishment by the CCD programs. That CCD might have more effect if there were considerable reinforcement of its work at home is probably true. But as we have seen already, only one-fourth of the Catholics in the United States came from families that provided reinforcement forceful enough to make the consequences of a comprehensive religious education impressive" (p. 191).

In addition to the fact that the loaded language of the opening sentence is a shade less than scientific objectivity, the authors do not seem to grasp the point here, and that is, that their own argument is two edged. It is precisely because three-fourths of families do not seem to profit from the vast expenditures of Catholic schools that many people feel that CCD should be given a chance to experiment and grow. The question once more is not whether a CCD school is a substitute for a Catholic school but whether a reassessment of the use of resources would give the CCD a fighting chance within a different educational structure. It is something other than "romance" that leads supporters of CCD to think that the dedicated people in this work deserve better than they are getting in terms of money, talent and energies. All the grand talk about the importance of the CCD is no substitute for the commitment of resources. At the recent inter-American congress of the CCD this crucial issue was not squarely faced.

It is clear that there is one decisive step needed at the moment to move us from dead center where we remain today. A way must be found to free money, manpower, talents and energies from the Catholic school system. If one keeps in mind the ambiguity that I spoke of at the beginning of this essay, then this proposal will not be interpreted as an attack upon the Catholic schools nor a cry for their liquidation. If we can be confident that we are not doing something bad in concentrating on the minority educated in Catholic schools, it is not a shocking or unrealistic proposal that we limit that minority still more.

This reduction would involve the relatively simple task of not expanding the system in most places and of concentrating on the quality of the teaching in the existing schools. Besides this consolidation it is imperative that some teachers be immediately released from Catholic schools for three main purposes. First, teachers must reach adults. One great potentiality of the Catholic school is the fact that it already has contact with the family through the school. Unfortunately, the possibilities for reaching the parents here have not often been utilized. This is not meant as a criticism of Catholic school teachers and administrators. While they have been under the pressure of continual expansion, they could hardly have been expected to lift their sights beyond the class room.

Second, teachers of religion must be given opportunities for further study. Formal religious instruction can generally be carried out in twentieth-century America only by people competently trained for the work. The heroic efforts of recent years to provide catechetical institutes and in-service training have been a great help but only a stop gap operation. Teachers should be given the possibility of a minimum of one full year of study in master's programs in this country or catechetical

143

centers in Canada, England and the continent. This has been happening by the ones, twos and dozens; it is needed by the hundreds and the thousands.

Third, teachers must be freed to work with students outside Catholic schools, especially on the college level. Some of the teachers already trained and some of those who will come back from study must be given a wider scope than the Catholic school program. What form their work may take has yet to be imagined. The beleaguered few in CCD and Newman have never had the luxury of thinking this program through, let alone accomplishing it.

If draining off some of the best catechetical talent from the Catholic schools seems to require that faculties there remain perilously thin, I would suggest that fewer courses of religion ought to be taught in Catholic schools. It is assumed that the purpose of Catholic schools is to give religious instruction and therefore as much religion as possible ought to be taught. I think that this is a fundamentally wrong principle and that this sociological study together with psychological and theological data would support my contention. We are still working on the supposition that if we throw enough doctrine and precept, some of it is bound to stick. More likely, however, the opposite is true. The more that students are run around the same circle—often by unenthusiastic or unprepared teachers—the more the students get convinced that we have nothing to say. By the time they get to college where one might begin to discuss Christianity as a religion for adults, they are oversaturated with technical words and undigested ideas that hinder learning. One sometimes has the frightening feeling that the modern catechetical movement with its elaborate new approaches on primary and secondary levels may only be exacerbating the situation.

The number of religion courses in grammar schools and high schools ought to be drastically reduced. This should not be done by dropping an hour here and there but by a complete overhaul of the system that will make clear what is being done. One or two very stimulating courses in the high school by teachers with adequate preparation would be more valuable than what is generally being done. Far from making useless the rest of the teachers in the Catholic school, this change would make it more evident that the whole school contributes to the religious development of students, though only a few do so as catechists.

When children are young they need an introduction to Christian living provided by the family and reinforced by early schooling. When people are reaching the stage of adult maturity they need intellectually challenging study of the Christian faith. In between these two stages children should simply be allowed to grow up. The Catholic school ought to provide a truly human and Christian atmosphere in which they can grow up. It is neither desirable nor feasible to close off the middle of the Catholic school system; but the school at this point would achieve a result as good if not better without formal religion teaching. The milieu is the chief formative influence as this study shows, and the function of the Catholic school at this level is to be a "citadel of charity" (Sloyan).

Enormous amounts of money and energy are currently going into projects to develop twelve-year religion programs for Catholic schools. This includes the writing of textbooks that will not bore to tears the children run through this cycle. Is this really necessary or helpful? Despite the subtlety and imagination of textbook writers, the students are not easily convinced that this is not the "same old stuff" dressed up with brighter pictures and newer words. I suggest that this is not the fault of the writers or the teachers but of the structure itself. Most of those doctrinal and ethical beliefs that we so laboriously strive to inject into fifth-graders or ninth-graders can be easily picked up by a college student or adult who is ready and desires to learn. The results of this sociological study should give us added confidence to experiment, knowing that no great calamities will ensue because students are taught fewer religion courses.

145

We must, therefore, move immediately to reduce the number of courses to coincide with the number of people having some competence to teach them. At the same time this would begin to free people, money and attention for other purposes.

The cry from some teachers that we do not have enough time now to cover all the material will surely be heard. It is an age-old cry of teachers, but one not relevant in this issue. Most students get convinced by the fourth or fifth grade that they have covered all the material and that the rest is repetition. Instead of teachers working feverishly to say it all again in a more interesting way, they ought to be reminded that the salvation of their students does not depend on covering all the material. Teachers could use some encouragement in realizing that they are making a small but valuable contribution if they can give to their students some enthusiasm and interest together with a serious learning challenge.

Any proposal to reorganize the total pattern of religious education may seem hopelessly naïve. Can such basic changes be made in an enormous system? I do not know. But I do know that it cannot be done without a structural and administrative realignment. There is a pressing need, in the first place, for some people in the country to be concerned with religious education as distinct from Catholic school and CCD offices. This would include a national coordinating agency adequately financed and drawing on the best talent in the country. Such a body would make use of all educational media for research, experimentation and direction. The national director would have to work with diocesan and sub-diocesan directors of religious education. There is need for a great coordination of effort to assure the wise and equitable use of available money. The problems in doing this are enormous, but the problems will never even be tackled until there is the conviction at every level that preference must be given to people rather than buildings, adults rather than children, and teacher training rather than catechisms.

My remarks here leave open to question the future of the Catholic schools. If Rossi and Greeley are correct, the Catholic schools are doing a creditable job and it is to be hoped that their work will be even better in the future. What the eventual role of the Catholic school will be can only be discovered as we gradually shift the orientation of our total educational effort. My suggestions for further questioning in this area not intended as a disparagement of the Greeley-Rossi study. These two men have tested the behavioral effects of Catholic education in the past and these results can be of great value for us. But the question that now needs asking, and which the sociologists did not or could not ask, is: When are we going to realize that Christianity is a religion for adults and begin to have the implications of this fact reflected in the allocation of resources?

147

11. Of Small Groups and Large Crowds

ONE OF the main themes throughout these essays has been that we are underrating the role of teaching and the value of intelligence in religious education. Teachers could make a small but significant contribution to Christian life if they would take their own role seriously. Instead, there is a strong tendency in schools to abandon the teaching of Christianity before it has really been tried. In place of intellectual learning many schools are trying to provide experiences in Christian living. Although I am not against religious experiences, the school may worsen its already shaky position by taking on more than it can handle. Much of what is being attempted in religion classes these days is artificial; some of it is frightening.

It is not enough, however, to assert this position and hope that other people will be convinced. One must go on to uncover the deep-seated reasons for this tendency in the schools today. The first and most evident reason is the continuing inadequacy of teacher preparation. Among those in authority there is still hardly a glimmer of realization of the magnitude of the problem. As long as teachers are inadequately trained for their task they will obviously have to substitute something else for good teaching. They will grasp at any straw that makes their situation bearable. Thus, theological education for teachers is obviously one part of the solution to this problem.

The answer, however, is not that simple. I am still convinced that intelligence and learning are the essence of religion teaching. Yet in talking with teachers I have been forced to question this presupposition. What has impressed me in visiting many schools recently has been the large number of young, competent and well-trained teachers who are having their problems. Many of them find the teaching of religion excruciatingly difficult. This is causing a frightening situation since some of those who could best do the job are the ones who are asking out of it.

There is only one conclusion that I can draw from this mass flight. There is a basic fault in the structure into which teachers are being fitted. Even the best of teachers finds himself at wit's end in trying to teach. He is forced into the exaggerated attempt at relevance. Religion classes are being taken half-way out of the classroom, a tactic that improves things for a while only to make them eventually worse. Keeping religion within the academic setting while eliminating all the academic criteria (tests, marks, homework, etc.) may in time produce impossible tensions. I am not saying whether religion ought to be in or out of the school; but I think it must be one or the other. In like manner, the injection of interesting, exciting or sensational material into religion teaching may also be a short term solution. The trouble with sensationalism is that appetites quickly become jaded, and unless the excitation value constantly goes up then worse boredom ensues.

The underlying difficulty that remains is that too many people who are in religion classes have no desire to be there and no wish to learn. It may be, as I indicated in the last essay, that Christianity is not something that should be studied each year in school. It might instead pertain to critical stages of intellectual growth. Good teachers and interesting material are not much help if the students do not really have the capacity for this learning. Many Catholic schools are in the process of dropping religion courses; some of them out of conviction, some of them with a sense of relief that they now have an excuse. Obviously, this reduction in the amount of teaching in Catholic schools is not the whole answer. In order to let the teachers teach we need a radical change of structure for religious education.

Religious education today ought to be aimed in two different

149

directions at the same time: toward very small groups and toward very large crowds. This principle may seem obvious but I maintain that we are now not aiming at either of these two audiences. Generally speaking, we are going right in between the two of them; the result is a very inefficient use of our precious resources for religious education. The fact that we are working at neither of the levels that desperately need attention is nobody's fault in particular. It is a result of the fact that much of our educational apparatus is left over from another century. The difficulties we are thus experiencing are shared by other educational agencies in modern society, but the difficulties are particularly acute for Christian religious education.

My principle is that our two chief concerns must be mass-media communication and small group learning. Many people have a feeling for one or the other of these two but few people appreciate the complementary character of these means. They are two different kinds of means but they necessarily go together. Those who are impressed by the effects of face-to-face encounter often overlook the magnitude of the world-wide problem and the stubbornness of powerfully established structures. Those whose minds are fascinated by the multitudes hope to reach them by spreading everything thinner with the result that no one is really reached. What I wish to stress in this essay is the different but complementary character of work with very small numbers and very large numbers.

There are psychological and technological reasons for this principle but there is also a deeper theological reason. The peculiar character of Christian love is that it is directed at one and the same time to the man who is closest and to the man who may be farthest away. The neighbor whom I am called to love is any stranger who happens to be in need. The neighbor is also anyone who belongs to the whole universal community of mankind. Every true love of an individual carries beyond itself to a love of all; similarly, hatred for any human being infects each individual relationship that is supposedly love.

Christ was not the first teacher to say that men should love; his unique doctrine was the indissoluble unity of love of God and love of neighbor, the expression of love of God through concrete acts of love of neighbor, and the union of all men in common sonship.

It could hardly be more erroneous than to suppose that Christianity means being nice (but not getting too involved) with a fairly large number of associates. The world has never lacked civic, tribal and national unities, but the gap between these groups and a universal community is not simply one of quantity. The unifying basis of these various groups stands at least in partial contradiction to the formation of a community of mankind. Christianity, therefore, does not try to enlarge these groupings, it reverses their principle of unity from one of defensiveness to one of love. Christianity makes its contribution to a world wide community by getting men deeply involved with the stranger next to them, so deeply that the universally human is unveiled in the exchange.

The principle is well illustrated by the two main directions for renewing the liturgy. For celebrating the Eucharist we need two quite distinct forms: one that is suitable for a few people around a table and one that is intended for a gigantic, solemn celebration. That we have neither of these forms is unfortunate though understandable; that we do not seem to be moving toward either form is exasperating. We are caught in a parochial structure in which the liturgy is multiplied for amorphous groups of people who will never develop a sense of liturgy under these conditions. What the church needs is on the one hand to carry out an infrequent but magnificent celebration and on the other hand to send the priests to wherever small communities of people are.

When I speak of small groups for liturgical experience there is no exact number of participants that can be specified. Other factors besides number enter into consideration. Six people do not always constitute a unit while twenty-five may feel closely

151

knit together by reason of the bonds of friendship, work or neighborhood. Nonetheless, there is an inescapable principle of size that must be considered. If one wishes to "encounter thou's" there are only a limited number of people that one can get deeply involved with at a particular time. This is a physical, psychological, social fact. The intense revelational and experiential function of liturgy can only be accomplished within a small community. This is not the whole meaning of liturgy but it is an indispensable part.

At the other end of the scale there is a different kind of celebration for a large congregation. This form is to serve the universalizing function of the liturgy which should not be overlooked today. Catholic tradition was not entirely wrong in its eye for the spectacle, the aesthetically magnificent production that draws men beyond themselves. There is still a place for this kind of assembly even though it is probably a lesser place. But it is important to realize that this is one kind of liturgy which can contribute to Christian life, provided that it is complemented by the small-group experience. In the largescale celebration, limitation of size is not desirable at all. The bigger the assembly is, the greater can be the witness to the universal character of Christianity. If there are going to be six hundred at the Eucharist, one might better have six thousand. Leadership of this assembly presumably would be a main function of the high priest of the community. If the pope cannot make it every year to great centers like New York or Chicago, maybe he could come every other year. At other times all the bishops of a region might lead their combined people in prayer. This suggestion may call to mind specters of a garrison church asserting its might and worldly power. That image does not necessarily follow. The church is already known for its power and riches; bringing together 50,000 of its people to confess their sins, pray for peace, and lift up their hearts, might have a good effect within the church and beyond it.

The last sentence touches on another liturgical act that would even better illustrate my principle. I mean the sacrament of penance. Statistics are not readily available but there is no doubt that sacramental confessions have gone into steep decline and that in some places the sacrament appears on the verge of extinction. This is most unfortunate since man is still a sinner and a liturgy of penance has not become outdated. However, the form which is still being clung to is hopelessly unsuited to the needs. As with the Eucharist, we need something deeply intimate that can only happen with an individual or a small group. We also need a large-scale communal expression of guilt and sorrow. With ministers of the sacrament forced to sit for hours in little boxes listening to mechanical formulas, there is no time or psychic energy to do the two things needed. The priest cannot minister to the deep problems of the individual, nor can he plan and execute a social celebration of penance by all of his people.

It is admittedly an immense task to develop the kind of liturgical expressions needed today. But these will never be developed if the church continues to aim almost exclusively at the middle-size congregations that fill and unfill the parking lots each Sunday morning. Many people are beginning to suspect that we are in the midst of a great liturgical crisis, a greater one than anybody could have predicted a few years ago. The attempt to update the liturgy has succeeded in revealing how out of date it was and still is. The first flush of successful change has been succeeded by a rather steady level of mediocrity. A radical transformation is urgently needed, and although the transformation cannot be immediately accomplished, the prerequisites for reform could be effected without delay. One of those prerequisites is the recognition of these two very different forms of liturgy which can accomplish two different things. Without this realization, the adaptations lead to incongruities and, when these are perfected, to absurdity. Anyone who

153

has been at small-group liturgies retaining the remnants of the other form (vestments, genuflections, sermons, etc.) knows what I mean.

When one turns to the more formal aspects of religious education, it is evident that the same two-pronged approach is needed. Unfortunately, it is also true here that most of the effort is being scattered at amorphous middle groups. There are many people working feverishly at the improvement of religious education and for this we must be grateful. But when they look up and realistically face the task of reaching the country's fifty million Catholics (not to mention the other one hundred fifty million non-Catholics with whom they should be concerned), there is likely to be frustration if not despair. Although the exact nature of the institutions we need is not clear to anyone, the principle I have enunciated above should be guiding our efforts. We must move toward educational organization that will efficiently reach millions of adults. The effect of a lecture or written essay or movie is limited but it can be real. Complementing this kind of education must be the occasions for intense theological learning or religious experiences provided for the small groups of adults who desire and are ready for this kind of thing.

Today's world is one of mass-media communication on a worldwide scale. We are not yet able even to imagine what this could mean for religious education. Never before in the history of Christianity has it been possible to speak the word to the ends of the world. The means are for the first time available to reach the entire human community. These fantastic possibilities will not be realized, however, without a great coordination of effort. There is need for a willingness to invest in people and in intelligent planning. Although many people are currently trying to get national coordination, it does not yet exist.

What does exist at present is an unbelievable proliferation of lecture series, institutes and catechetical days that are not coordinated at all. Each of these projects may seem to be a worthwhile venture but the total effort is hardly the way to work efficiently in contemporary America. We have few enough speakers and writers of outstanding ability; we have even fewer creative thinkers. If we do not stop flying these people around the country to give one-hour lectures in small auditoriums, we shall soon have none. Men who are going to speak well or write well need time, physical and psychical energy, and opportunity for their own studies. With proper organization they could get these and what they produce could reach thousands or millions of people. As it is now, erratic writing is dispersed in erratic fashion, and speakers burn themselves out in trying to answer the impossible demands made upon them. The American church can place second to none the question of means of communication on a national scale.

The limited effect that can be achieved by mass media must be complemented by the work of small groups. These could be concerned specifically with theological learning or with a kind of "Christian life experience" broadly educational in character. In either case the limitation of size for these groups is even more severe than in the case of the liturgy. When there are more than seven or eight people around a table they are no longer talking to each other and learning together. Small-group learning has a possible effectiveness that is beyond measure. However, it requires some faith and some patience to achieve this effectiveness. All too often we are vague on the nature of this task and the result is a holding on to dead forms from another kind of operation. For example, we think of doubling the group to double our effectiveness; instead we destroy the whole thing. Or else we grow impatient and feel it is not worth the effort and the time to work with six when there are six thousand more to reach. Our mistake is in thinking that if six out of six thousand come we are working at one thousandth of the educational problem, whereas in fact we have already begun to solve one half of the problem. Priests, reli-

155

gious or teachers are never going to get to the fifty million, but small groups of lay adults, once they have been deeply affected, will reach out toward the whole population.

Some people may object that such small groups have long existed in the church and have not produced these startling results. It is true that the effect of even the best of these groups has been very limited. Part of the reason for this is that the complementary pole, mass-media communication, has been inadequate. Part of the reason, too, is that work with the small group of adults has been peripheral in the educational work of the church. The manpower, money, talent and interest have been elsewhere. It is time to start taking with utter seriousness what has been discovered outside the church: the dynamic power of small-group learning. What we need are professionally competent people who understand the dynamics of the learning situation. Simply having sessions on group interaction may be the first step for many people in the church, including and perhaps especially those thought to be the teachers. The fact that these training sessions at the beginning are completely secular or non-religious may be to their advantage. Christianity is not interested in inserting religious motivations but it is concerned with unleashing human capabilities. When some of the blocks to affection, freedom and open-mindedness are removed, real theological inquiry might begin.

This demand for group specialists may seem hopelessly unrealistic. We are having trouble enough in finding religion teachers with a minimal degree of competence to teach religion. My proposal, however, is not simply to place additional burdens on the already overworked structure. It is to coordinate, consolidate and redirect our efforts. Instead of trying to fill classrooms with competent teachers we ought to have the very competent lecturers speaking to thousands or millions. In turn that would free many teachers to work with six or eight people. This would be both more effective and less exhausting. In addition, it would uncover a whole new pool of educators. There are many people who cannot survive at the front of a religion classroom but who could function well with a few people in an informal learning experience.

If what I have said so far has general validity, there is one big step that is needed now. Every large urban area needs one or more centers for religious education. Such a center should cut across parochial lines; in a few instances it might cut across diocesan boundaries. The important thing is that it be where the people are. The center must be designed for two purposes: it must on the one hand be equipped for mass communication (television, film, mass distribution of literature, huge lecture hall); on the other hand, it must be suitable as living space for small group learning. Although presumably conducted by Catholics, it would be ecumenical to its roots simply because it would be so open to all modes of learning.

There are only a few dioceses in the country that have a center like this and in most of those places it is at the periphery of education. The kind of center I am suggesting requires not just approval but support, backing and encouragement by diocesan officials. There is no way for a few concerned Catholics to initiate such a thing; it cannot be done without some leadership at the top. Any big investment to produce the top-flight centers we need must be carefully planned and these will take years to build. But it is entirely feasible to suggest that less elaborate versions of the model could be started this year. If the conviction were there at the top, a few strokes of the pen could set the machinery going.

The kind of center eventually to be built would be a real center of operations, a place where something would be happening every day at every hour. It would be the place where all that is best in religious publishing would be accessible and where the audio-visual world could come into its own. Outstanding lectures would be available to the public or specialized lectures would be given, for example, to update the clergy of the area. Facilities for small-group activities would be an important part. These would range from seminar rooms for discussions to living quarters for extended retreats or therapy sessions. In short, this would be a place for a Christian adult. A national resource center and a national coordinating agency are obviously part of the picture. This means not a superorganization but a group of intelligent and educated people who are given backing in their attempts at coordination. The institutionalization on a national level would arise from these people and be at their service.

The local establishment of a center for religious education would not be a financial burden. Over a period of time it would reduce the amount of money being spent on religious education. It is difficult to see how a diocese could make a mistake in spending its money this way. On the other hand, it is very difficult to understand why in preference to a center, a diocese would contemplate a new multi-million dollar school. Such a choice to build one more school in a hopeless race against increasing numbers of children would seem to be grotesquely outdated. This last remark prescinds entirely from the question of the quality of Catholic schools or the present state of CCD. The question posed here is how to make effective use of our resources in the future. The burning issue is not Catholic school or CCD but the education of the entire Catholic population.

I have not relinquished the position with which this essay began, namely, that religious education should concentrate on teaching and learning. My contention is, however, that it is nearly impossible to teach Christianity to children within our present structure. Worse still, our determined efforts to master the impossible prevent us from even getting to larger issues. A reorientation of effort on a national scale is urgently necessary before our resources are hopelessly dispersed.